# HOW TO PRUNE WESTERN SHRUBS

*By*

## R. SANFORD MARTIN

*Publisher*

*Illustrated by the Author*

*Exclusive Distributors to the Book Trade*

## MURRAY & GEE, INC.

3630 Eastham Drive
CULVER CITY, CALIFORNIA

THE PRESS OF MURRAY & GEE, INC.— CULVER CITY

# Contents

# FOREWORD

●

IN the publication of this book, I have endeavored to help that person who takes interest in the proper care of trees and shrubs, to get greater beauty and longer life from them through the medium of correct pruning. I have tried to make the wording and illustrations as simple and practical as possible to avoid confusion.

The majority of ornamental trees and shrubs, where grown for the beauties of their bloom or foliage effects, will be greatly improved if consistently pruned in order to develop their greatest natural beauty or to prolong their normal span of usefulness. The methods suggested in the following pages, for the pruning of your shrubs, are the results of several years of experiment, practice and observation throughout the Pacific coast area. Realizing full well the tendency of the average plant lover's abhorrence to cut a plant that is admired, I know that some of the readers of these instructions will have grave doubts about the outcome of such methods as I have suggested. However, the pruning that is recommended has been proven, and where I have stated that severe cutting is necessary, I have not done so without the knowledge that this heavy cutting is going to be of definite benefit to the plant, and its flowering abilities.

The illustrations, as one may readily see, are not intended to be works of art, but are kept as simple as possible, the more perfectly to convey the idea of *how* and *where* to cut. The plants pictured are not perfect specimens, but only "skeleton" types, to show what to cut and what to leave.

In the Pacific coast area, particularly in Southern

7

California, shrubs are very apt to make exceptionally rapid growth where they are raised under our average yard conditions, so that correct pruning becomes a most essential practice in order to continue the maximum beauty of these shrubs. There has been entirely too much butchering and hedging of plants, and when this crude cutting is done, the natural beauty of a plant has been temporarily destroyed. Every ornamental shrub has some height at which it attains its greatest beauty, so with the system of pruning that is recommended for these plants, I have endeavored to govern their care in order that they may be maintained at this stage throughout their entire life.

— R. SANFORD MARTIN.

# How to Prune Western Shrubs

•

## ABELIA GRANDIFLORA (Rupestris)
## GLOSSY ABELIA

This shrub has a very long blooming period naturally and will produce an abundance of flowers every year if cared for properly. It is the nature of this plant to pro-

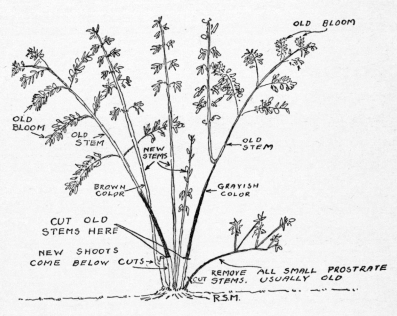

OLD BLOOM

OLD BLOOM

OLD STEM

NEW STEMS

OLD STEM

BROWN COLOR

GRAYISH COLOR

CUT OLD STEMS HERE

NEW SHOOTS COME BELOW CUTS →

CUT

REMOVE ALL SMALL PROSTRATE STEMS. USUALLY OLD

R.S.M.

ABELIA GRANDIFLORA
(RUPESTRIS)

duce its best flowers on branches that are one year old, so for the best results it is advisable to keep as much of this new growth coming along as is possible.

9

The correct time of year for pruning this variety is during the winter months, while the plant is dormant. It will be noticed that the branches that supported the flowering twigs are of a slightly grayish coloring. These are the ones to be cut out. Cut these branches at their base, about eight inches from the ground, and the new growth will start below this cut. These new shoots will produce blossoms after they have had one complete season of growing. Don't make the mistake of cutting these branches high above the ground, because the new growth will be concentrated just below where the cut was made, so if cut too high, the plant will soon become top-heavy.

This variety of Abelia should not require pruning until it has had three summers' growth.

At the time of year when the pruning should be done the branches to be left will be a decided brown in color and will produce the best flowers the following summer. If any of these brown shoots should have started more than one foot from the ground, do not hesitate to remove them when the older wood is cut out. Plenty of new growth will appear in good time to produce an abundance of bloom.

## ABUTILON, FLOWERING MAPLE

There are two systems of pruning this tree-shrub, and it depends somewhat upon the locality in which the plant has been used, as to which method would be best.

In case the shrub is planted in a mild frost-free locality, it will act as an evergreen, which, by the way, is not its nature, and by careful pruning may be kept in bloom almost the entire year. For this type, a system of thinning out is the proper procedure, and may be done every three months throughout the year. When allowed to go un-cut, this plant becomes very ungainly or spindling, and as the blooms appear upon new wood only, the longer branches should be headed back in order to force new growth from the base of these same branches. Make the cuts well down into the body of the plant, and this reduction of top will force new growth elsewhere, bringing with it new flowering wood.

Where a plant goes completely dormant during the winter months, it may be dehorned, or stubbed back heavily during the winter. This will cause the plant to put out a wonderfully luxuriant growth, of large leaves

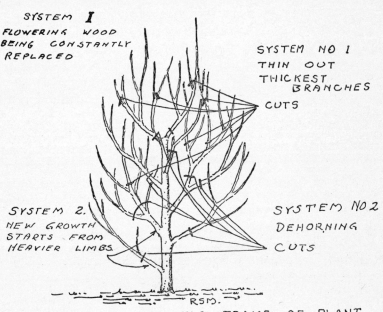

SYSTEM I
FLOWERING WOOD
BEING CONSTANTLY
REPLACED

SYSTEM NO I
THIN OUT
THICKEST
BRANCHES
CUTS

SYSTEM 2.
NEW GROWTH
STARTS FROM
HEAVIER LIMBS

SYSTEM NO 2
DEHORNING
CUTS

RSM.

ABUTILON — SHOWING FRAME OF PLANT AND CUTS TO BE MADE.

and longer stemmed flowers. A heavy cutting of this sort may be done every year without damaging the plant in the least, in fact its normal life of beauty will be prolonged.

Where the former method is employed, it will be found that the plant can be kept at about a six to eight foot height indefinitely.

If the plant has been frosted during the winter, cut back at least two inches beyond any frosted discolorations that may appear on the stems.

## ADENDROCARPUS VISCOSUS, CANARY ISLAND LUPINE

Pruning of this free blooming shrub should not become necessary until the plant is at least four years old, and then all that will be needed is a general thinning out of the oldest erect and arching branches. This work should be done in early spring after the frosts have passed, but before the spring growing period starts.

Correct pruning will benefit this plant by keeping a new supply of main branches, upon which the flowers appear in short lateral spikes. After one of these main branches has become over three years old, they will develop open, leafless spaces in their lower areas, which makes a very unsightly shrub, and this system of pruning will correct the condition.

When pruning becomes necessary do not cut out branches too freely. Select one or two of the oldest, coarsest branches and cut them out about eight inches from their base. Then remove any low, older branches which have gradually lowered to the ground. These lower branches contribute little to the plant, because they receive little or no direct sunlight, and as a result produce few flowers or foliage.

The following year take out one or two more of the oldest branches in the above manner, and so on every spring. This system will cause the plant to produce an abundance of bloom on well leafed branchlets.

The seed should be picked off as it is formed, causing a tendency to produce more and better flowers.

## ALMOND, FLOWERING

This attractive little spring flowering shrub is one that will need little care, except the replenishing of its flower bearing wood.

The blooms appear in the spring on wood that is at least one year old, and will bloom again on this same branch, so it will not be necessary to keep cutting out the past season's wood every year. As the plant grows older some of the oldest branches will become rather coarse, shy of foliage and flowers. These branches should be removed in the spring, as soon as the crop of flowers has dropped. Cut the branches that have become ragged almost to the ground, and new shoots will develop below this cut.

In picking sprays of bloom for the house, it would be advisable to select those of the older branches. When cutting this wood, treat the plant the same as though it were being pruned.

Old plants of this variety will have many branches starting from the base, and almost sprawling on the ground. These should be trimmed off entirely, leaving but a very short stub at the base.

## ALTHAEA, HIBISCUS SYRIACUS
## ROSE OF SHARON

This group of shrubs will need but little pruning because of the fact that they are slow growers, and of a good even development. During the winter months, while the plant is leafless, will be the best time of year to do any cutting that is necessary. On the average plant, because of its slow development, pruning will only be needed about every three years, and then a simple thinning out process.

About every three years, it is advisable to reshape this plant by cutting out any branches that have grown in such a manner as to interfere with one another. Do not just cut off the tips, but take out the entire interfering branch because the majority of flowers are borne at the ends of the branches, and tip cutting would merely stop any bloom on that branch and not remedy the interference that the branch has caused.

By keeping the shrub well opened up, allowing the sunlight to penetrate to the inner part of the plant, the flowers will be of a better quality. If the location in which the plant has been set will permit, it would be

13

advisable to not let the topmost branches grow over six feet tall at any time. By keeping the tallest branches thinned out one may keep the size of the plant down to this height.

## ARBUTUS UNEDO, STRAWBERRY TREE

When this shrub is used as a natural growing plant in mass planting, it will require very little pruning. It should be planted where it can develop naturally without interference from anything else around it. But when it has been planted in a location where it cannot be permitted to become tall, the plant may be kept within control very easily by a thinning out process.

The shrub will usually have developed from one to three main stems, and these should be kept for the framework of the plant. When branches become too tall for the location, they may be cut back by selecting several from different parts of the plant, and cutting them back to within about four or five inches from their base. By selecting these branches from different parts of the plant, their being removed will not leave a "hole" in any one side. These branches being cut back will cause new shoots to develop throughout the entire plant, which will quickly hide any signs of cutting.

Do not attempt to trim this plant as you would a hedge, as this treatment will merely concentrate the growth where the trimming was done, and in a very short time the growth will be worse than before.

Pruning may be done during the winter or early spring months. Do not do any cutting while the plant is in bloom, as that would cause many of the beautiful fruit to be removed.

## ASPIDISTRA

Strictly a house plant, or for very shady locations. Practically the only care necessary for this plant is to cut off the leaves at the surface of the ground as they be-

14

come discolored with old age. These plants are excellent pot or tub plants, and when they become too large for their container, may either be transferred to a larger container or subdivided into smaller divisions. This operation, however, should be done by a nurseryman who is familiar with this plant, as they are not the easiest plant to transplant. They are quite often killed in subdividing. It would be advisable to leave the plant with the nurseryman for about a month after transplanting, in order to insure proper attention.

About every three or four weeks the leaves should be wiped off on both sides with a moist cloth in order to insure proper breathing of the plant. This is very important where the plant is being kept indoors.

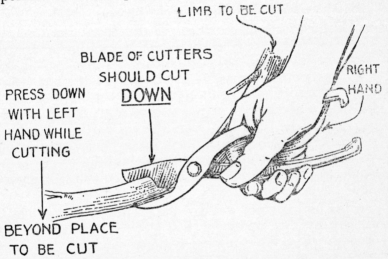

LIMB TO BE CUT

BLADE OF CUTTERS
SHOULD CUT
**DOWN**

RIGHT HAND

PRESS DOWN
WITH LEFT
HAND WHILE
CUTTING

BEYOND PLACE
TO BE CUT

THE EASIEST WAY TO
MAKE HEAVY CUTS.

## AUCUBA JAPONICA

Strictly a shade loving plant requiring little pruning of any kind. These plants are sometimes inclined to become too spindling, throwing all their energy into the one central growth. This may be overcome by pinching out the terminal, or end bud, which will force new growth along the main stem.

If the plant has not shown signs of branching by the time it is twenty inches tall, it would be advisable to nip out the terminal bud. This may be done at any time of the year.

## BELOPERONE GUTTATA, SHRIMP PLANT, ETC.

This fast growing plant will need some pruning attention about once a month during the summer season in order to keep it as its best, and to lengthen its natural span of usefulness.

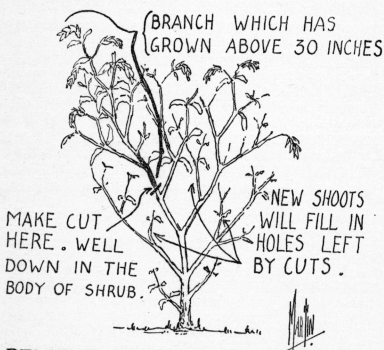

(BRANCH WHICH HAS GROWN ABOVE 30 INCHES

MAKE CUT HERE. WELL DOWN IN THE BODY OF SHRUB.

NEW SHOOTS WILL FILL IN HOLES LEFT BY CUTS.

BELOPERONE . SHRIMP PLANT . PRUNE WHEN EVER NECCESSARY ALL DURING GROWING SEASON .

The pruning system is simple, but very important, and must be attended to at regular intervals for the best results. Unlike most plants, the pruning must be done all during the growing and flowering period, which in mild locations will be every month of the year.

Due to the weak structure of the plant's stems, it is advisable to not allow the shrub to attain more than a thirty inch height. The system of pruning recommended will have a tendency to make a broader shrub with greater flowering area.

When a branch attains its height of thirty inches, it should be removed by following down the stem to about one foot from the ground and cutting the branch off about one-half inch above a joint. New shoots will be forced from every joint below the cut, which will produce flowers in a short time. In removing this tall branch, other lateral branches of the one to be removed will have to be sacrificed too, but the plant will recover so rapidly that it will not matter for long. Also, if too many branches are left in the top of the plant, it will soon become top-heavy, and will require staking, which is not good practice.

Other varieties of Beloperone, with the pink and lavendar flowers will require a general thinning out about once a year, in the spring, before the growing season starts.

## BERBERUS, BARBERRY

This is a plant that is usually used in mass planting or as a hedge, and in either case little or no pruning is found necessary, but where it is used as a specimen plant you will find that any of the varieties of the Barberry group may be kept looking very much more attractive when properly cut.

Where one of these plants is in a location permitting plenty of spread, it is advisable to keep the oldest wood cut out, allowing the new shoots or suckers to take its place, thus insuring a more graceful habit of growth, more bloom and berries. When the oldest branches begin to lose their attractiveness, they should be cut off close to the ground, leaving short stubs about six inches long on which the new wood will start. These shoots will have better foliage, more flowers and berries than the older branches.

This cutting should be done during the winter months while the plant is practically dormant. Some of the varieties make excellent Christmas decorations, so they may be pruned at that time of the year and the branches used in the house. It should not be necessary to prune any of the Barberries until they are four years old or more.

## BRUNFELSIA, YESTERDAY AND TODAY

Pruning of this colorful shrub should be attended to during the late winter months while the plant is not growing and should be done with the idea of producing new growth throughout the entire plant. The best bloom appears on the current season's growth, or that which grows this year, so any pruning done during the growing months would sacrifice bloom.

It is the nature of this plant to develop quite a tangle of branches during one summer, so to prune the shrub while dormant in late winter, thin out much of the last season's growth until there is an even distribution of branch growth over the entire plant. Depending upon the age of the shrub, this winter pruning should cut the plant back to about two feet, in a young plant, or to about four foot height in an older one.

If a good substantial foundation of branches is maintained with the Brunfelsia, staking will be unnecessary in order to control its growth. After the spring growth starts, new buds will be forced out any place on the old branches, so it is not essential to make a cut directly above an established bud or branch.

This system will apply to all varieties of this shrub now grown in this country.

## BUDDLEA, BUTTERFLY BUSH

There are three popular varieties of this shrub, but all may be treated the same as far as pruning is concerned. The main thing to remember with any of this group is to do the pruning as soon as the plant has stopped blooming, whether they be the summer flowering type or the

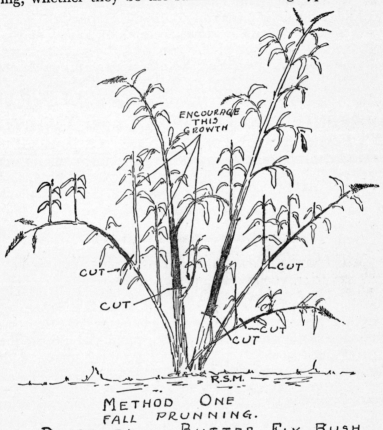

METHOD ONE
FALL PRUNNING.
BUDDLEA — BUTTER FLY BUSH

winter blooming. Cut them back as soon as they have finished flowering.

These plants are all such vigorous growers that they require severe cutting to keep them at their best. Normally, one of these plants may put out six feet or more growth each year. It is best to select about three of the main stems, and cut them back to about three feet from the ground. These stems will be the foundations of your plant in years to come. Cut all other growth to very short stubs. This will, of course, leave a very bare plant for a while, but it is necessary if one wants the largest possible flowers from this shrub.

The summer flowering blue Buddlea, where it is planted in a frost free location, can be made to bloom almost the entire year by thinning out only the oldest wood about every three months. This keeps the new growth coming along all the time, producing flowers much more than it would naturally. The writer has kept this type in bloom twelve months of the year by this method.

The *Evergreen Buddlea* should be thinned out twice a year rather sparingly, and the best times to do this would be January and June.

## BUXUS, BOXWOOD
## (Japanese and English)

Boxwoods are very apt to spindle out under favorable growing conditions and become open in growth, which is not desirable for these plants. Cut or trim the tips of the twigs on the outside of the plant, and this will force new growth on the inside, filling out the open holes. Continue this treatment until the plant is well filled out.

Where Boxwood plants are grown in pots or tubs, it is necessary to keep the plant rotating from time to time, to prevent burning on one side. About once a month give the pot a quarter turn, always in the same direction, and this will prevent the plant becoming one sided, or shy of leaves on one side.

The true Dwarf English Box is quite rare in this country, but it will grow indefinitely without any pruning whatsoever. This type often takes twenty years to attain a height of eighteen inches.

# CALLIANDRA, TRINIDAD FLAME BUSH

This is a plant that likes plenty of room to spread, and little can be done to improve its flowering ability or general shape as far as pruning is concerned. As long as there is plenty of sunshine, this shrub will bloom heavily on new or old branches.

The only pruning that should be necessary would be to remove any crossing or interfering stems, or cut out any branches that tend to make the branch one sided or unshapely. This pruning may be done at any time of the year, when it becomes necessary.

## CALLISTEMON, BOTTLE BRUSH

The majority of these plants are very slow growers and as a result require little or no pruning, except to prevent the shrub becoming one sided, or too thick and tangled. If the branches are kept open, there will be a much greater chance for heavy bloom.

It seems to be the nature of this plant to become gnarled, particularly the "rigidus" variety, so to avoid this habit, cut out any branches that show the tendency of interfering with one another in growth. Keep the branches thinned out to the extent of their being evenly distributed throughout the entire plant.

Where a plant begins to grow one sided, due to being planted too close to some object, or another plant, the whole shrub may be straightened by cutting out some of the growth on the side that is heaviest, which will cause new branches to develop on the light side.

Pruning on these plants may be done during the late fall or winter. By keeping the shrub well opened up there will be less chance of die-back, which is caused by too heavy massing of branch growth.

# CALYCANTHUS FLORIDUS, SWEET SHRUB

On the west coast, this plant takes on rather rank growing habits, and should be thinned out regularly for the best results. The oldest branches of this plant will become shy of foliage and bloom after a few seasons' growth, and as this condition arises these branches should be removed by cutting them out well down towards the base of the plant, leaving a stub at the end about one foot long. New shoots will sprout from this stub, which will form the framework for new flowering wood.

Pruning should be done during the winter months while the plant is free of foliage. This heavy cutting should not be needed more than once every two or three years.

## CAMELLIA JAPONICA

This is one tree-shrub that practically takes care of

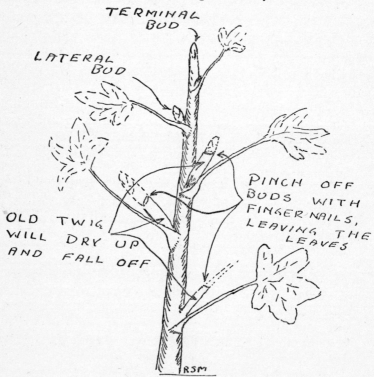

TERMINAL BUD

LATERAL BUD

PINCH OFF BUDS WITH FINGER NAILS, LEAVING THE LEAVES

OLD TWIG WILL DRY UP AND FALL OFF

HOW TO "PINCH OUT" BUDS.

itself as to pruning, and the only thing that may be done in this direction, is to prevent the growth from becoming one-sided, which might be due to the location in which the plant has been placed. So many of these plants are placed very close in on the north side of a house or wall, that the tendency is for the new growth to pull away, seeking the light. When this happens, cut off the branches that are contributing to the one sided appearance.

Camellias do not require a great deal of fertility and it is usually a mistake to put manure of any kind on the ground around them. Black Peat will give them all the fertility that is needed, and also supply the necessary acidity that is required by the roots.

## CANDOLLEA

This shrub will require little pruning as far as bloom improvement is concerned, but because of its growth habit, it will become necessary to remove the old, outer branches as they are no longer needed on the plant.

The Candollea is constantly replacing its branches from the inside of the plant, and as these branches grow and develop, they are gradually crowded out and down, until they practically touch the ground. As these branches become too low to be of use to the shrub, they should be cut off at their base, which will divert energy to other, more productive branches on the plant. This pruning may be done at any time of the year that it becomes necessary.

## CANTUA BUXIFOLIA and BICOLOR

This being a rather tender plant, and one that is easily affected by frosts, it sometimes does not survive sufficient winters to require pruning, but where it has been planted in a mild location, it may be carried on for many years.

It is advisable to drive a stake near the center of the plant for it to be trained upon, as the branches are of insufficient natural strength to support their own weight.

The flower producing branches will bear a good show-ing of flowers for several years, but due to the fact that after these branches are more than two years old they become very shy of leaves, it is better to keep new wood coming along from the base of the plant. After the erect flower producing branches have had two summers of growth, they should be cut out, almost to the ground, leaving a stub about six inches long. The new flowering wood will appear on these stubs.

This pruning should be done as soon as the plant has stopped blooming, in order to get a full season's growth on the branches that are to bear the new crop of blos-soms. Where this system is carried out every year, there will always be an ample supply of flower producing branches.

## CARISSA GRANDIFLORA
## NATAL PLUM

Although this is a fruit producing shrub, it is of suffi-cient beauty to be used frequently as an ornamental plant. However, it is one that requires very little in the way of pruning, except in the very early years of its growth, when it shows the tendency to sprawl out on the ground.

For the sake of a more permanently strong plant, do not attempt to stake up these low growing branches. Cut them off where they leave the main stem of the shrub, because as the plant grows older these first low growing branches will not be of any use, the fruit appearing on branches higher up. The shrub will not fruit until it is a few years old, so removing these low sprawling branches will not affect the fruiting ability in the least, but merely forces the growth into the top where the fruit will appear later.

Old plants are very apt to send out irregular growth, causing them to have a more one-sided appearance, and this may be overcome by cutting off any such growth where it leaves the body of the plant.

Pruning may be done in the Spring for the best results.

Because of the nature of the plant it is a mistake to attempt to stake it, but the shape should be developed through proper balancing by pruning.

## CASSIA, SENNA

The most popular varieties, such as tomentosa, nairobensis, and corymbosa, should be cut back heavily every year in order to prolong the natural beauty of this family of plants. As they produce their flowers on wood that is one season old, this wood should be kept developing for best results, by the following system of pruning:

The first year that the plant is set out, as soon as the flowers have dropped, cut the main stem down to about two or three feet from the ground. New shoots will then

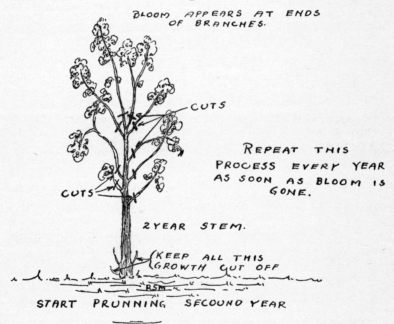

BLOOM APPEARS AT ENDS OF BRANCHES.

CUTS

REPEAT THIS PROCESS EVERY YEAR AS SOON AS BLOOM IS GONE.

CUTS

2 YEAR STEM.

KEEP ALL THIS GROWTH CUT OFF

RSM

START PRUNNING SECOUND YEAR

CASSIA TOMENTOSA

start out from below this cut, and will have ample time to develop new flowering wood by next season's blooming period. The next year, and every year following, as soon as the flowers are past, cut all of these one year growths back to short stubs of about three buds, or leaf scars, in length.

This severe cutting will of course leave the plant bare, but only for a short time, as its recovery is rapid. All of this family are inclined to become very spindling with age, but this system of cutting will keep them a beautiful plant year after year.

The Cassia artemesoides should not be treated as the above varieties, due to its different type of growth. As this plant becomes ungainly with age, the longest branches should be thinned out, removing them at their base, leaving short stubs for the development of new wood. This cutting should be done during the winter months, as it is a heavy summer bloomer. When doing the pruning, do not remove more than one-third of the branches in any one season.

## CEANOTHUS
## CALIFORNIA WILD LILAC

Practically no pruning will be necessary on the slower growing types of this plant, except to cut back any branches that have a tendency to over balance the shrub.

The faster growing types, such as cyaneous, thrysiflorus, etc., where they are grown under the average home yard condition, will develop very rapidly, and grow out of bounds in two or three seasons. When this occurs they must be cut back by a gradual thinning out process, because heavy cutting will sometimes cause a sour-sap condition, with ultimate death to the shrub. Whatever pruning is done, to keep the plant within desired limits, should be done at several times during the year, and in this way the plant will never have the appearance of being cut. The heaviest cutting may be done in the late fall, at which time the plants are practically dormant.

After these have become thoroughly established in their new location, do not give them very much water. By nature they are a very drought resistant plant, and they will produce many more flowers when allowed to go quite dry.

## CERCIS CANADENSIS, REDBUD

This plant may be treated as either a low tree or a rank shrub. A good deal will depend, of course, on the location of the plant already in your yard.

If the plant has been allowed to take its natural course, there will very likely be a mass of branches, with no definite shape to the whole plant. In this case, a good thinning will aid the plant in many ways. When doing this work, select some of the largest branches throughout the shrub and cut them out. Take out enough of these to open up the center of the plant and allow the sunlight to penetrate.

Where it is possible, this plant makes an excellent small tree, and it is quite easy to train this shrub in this manner. It will stand a four foot heading, and for further training treat it the same as one would any other shade tree. This work is covered under the heading of "Shade Trees." Lower branches will be inclined to droop while the plant is young, and these should be cut off. Suckers should be kept off at the base of the trunk. Cut these off smooth where they leave the root-stock.

## CESTRUM ELEGANS, AURANTIACUM PARQUI

The first two named varieties are those that respond most favorably to pruning, and it should be remembered that the best flowers, fruit and foliage will be borne on wood that is only one year old. Therefore it is advisable to keep this new growth coming along all of the time.

All three of these varieties will form suckers from the base of the plant readily, and these same suckers will produce the finest flowers and berries. When the plant is allowed to grow untrimmed, it soon becomes unsightly and shy of bloom, but where proper cutting back is carried on consistently, the plant may be kept the same size

every year, and loaded with flowers and berries. As soon
as the branch or shoot has had one complete season of
flowering, it should be removed, by cutting out at the
base, leaving about a six inch stub, for the development
of the new flowering wood.

The best time of the year to do this cutting is in the
very early spring, just before the spring growth is about
to start.

Unless it is absolutely necessary do not tie these

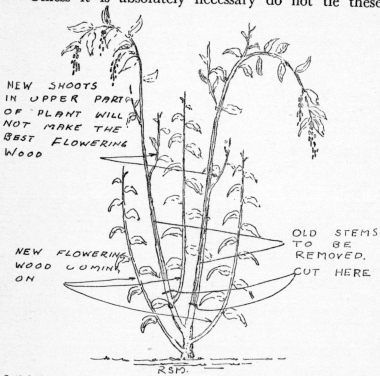

NEW SHOOTS IN UPPER PART OF PLANT WILL NOT MAKE THE BEST FLOWERING WOOD

OLD STEMS TO BE REMOVED. CUT HERE

NEW FLOWERING WOOD COMING ON

CESTRUM. SHOWING TYPICAL GROWTHS

branches up to a stake, as this treatment robs them of
their natural gracefulness. The new shoots will have
strength enough of their own to maintain an upright posi-
tion for the one season. The natural weight of the berries
will cause these branches to arch considerably, but this
feature is one of the main beauties of the plant.

## CHAMAELAUCIUM— GERALDTON WAX FLOWER

This free growing and free blooming shrub will take on a rather ungainly proportion as it grows older, so that it will become necessary to reshape the plant frequently.

Flowers are borne on current season wood or branches which grow this year, so the best time to do the pruning

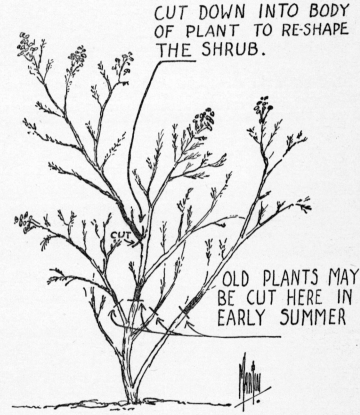

CUT DOWN INTO BODY OF PLANT TO RE-SHAPE THE SHRUB.

CUT

OLD PLANTS MAY BE CUT HERE IN EARLY SUMMER

CHAMAELAUCIUM . GERALDTON WAX FLOWER

is in early spring, while the sap is active within the stems. Make whatever cuts are necessary to re-shape the plant, without regard to lateral branches. New buds will be forced on the old stems, as needed by the plant.

In the case of old plants that have long since outgrown their location, very severe cutting, or dehorning may be done without danger. When this becomes necessary simply cut the whole top of the shrub off, about two feet from the ground. This severe dehorning should be done in early summer, while the scp is active. New shoots will form on the remaining stems, below the cuts, and during the next few months an entire new plant will be formed.

## CHOISYA TERNATA, MEXICAN ORANGE

This being a very dense growing shrub, it requires considerable patience to prune it properly, and not ruin the blooming possibilities, as one is apt to do if he trims this plant hedge fashion. The flowers of this plant appear at the terminal of the branch, and where the plant is growing too tall, this branch may be thinned out, as soon as its blossoming period has passed. The best time of the year to do this cutting will be late summer.

By keeping the shrub somewhat thinned out, one can not only give the plant greater flowering possibilities, but also preserve greater individuality for the plant itself. Select several branches throughout the entire plant, but not from any one area, and cut them out, well down into the center of the shrub. Take out enough to allow some direct sunlight to penetrate. Where sunlight is allowed to get to the inside, new growth will start on the inner portion of the plant, which will make more desirable flowering wood than that produced from continued terminal growth.

The flowers of the Choisya are very useful for large bouquets, and when cutting them for this purpose, be sure and keep this system of pruning in mind, even though longer stems are taken than would have been needed for the bouquet.

Keep this plant open in growth, and do not allow it

to become too tall. Five to six feet is plenty of height for this shrub to handle satisfactorily.

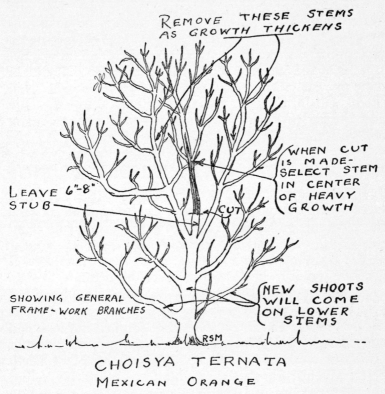

CHOISYA TERNATA
MEXICAN ORANGE

## CHORIZEMA ILLICIFOLIA and VARIUM

Either of these two types of Chorizema can be helped but little by any system of pruning. In the majority of cases, they are of a rather short life.

The production of seed is always a drain on any plant, so with this variety, if the seed is removed as soon as it is formed, it will put greater vitality in the body of the plant, especially the foliage. Each branchlet will have a long spike of flowers at the end, and as soon as these flowers are passed, the whole branchlet may be cut back about one-third of its length. This treatment will cause the plant to become a little more bushy, and thereby set a greater amount of bloom for the next season.

## CISTUS, ROCK ROSE

Although there are several varieties of this beautiful plant, the same system of cutting may be applied to all. They being a family of rather hard wooded plants, it is

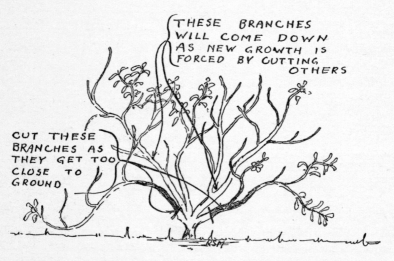

NEW SHOOTS WILL COME ON STUBS LEFT, WHICH REPLACE OLD GROWTH

THESE BRANCHES WILL COME DOWN AS NEW GROWTH IS FORCED BY CUTTING OTHERS

CUT THESE BRANCHES AS THEY GET TOO CLOSE TO GROUND

CISTUS — ROCK ROSE

not natural for them to throw out sucker growth after severe cutting, so any pruning has to be of a rather mild nature, and spread out over a prolonged period.

As a family they are inclined to grow somewhat one sided, or irregular, and this tendency may be overcome by thinning out the small branches in the heavier areas, which will in turn force new growth of wood in the parts of the plant less thickly covered with foliage.

The flowers of this plant are borne on fairly new wood, so it is of advantage to keep this type of wood constantly developing by thinning out the older, sparsely leaved branches. This cutting may be done throughout the entire year, but it is best to do the heaviest cutting during the winter months.

Do not allow these plants to be very moist, as a condition of this sort will cause them to grow too much to leaves with very few blooms.

## COPROSMA, WAX PLANT, LOOKING ..... GLASS PLANT, ETC.

One of the most commonly used ornamental shrubs,

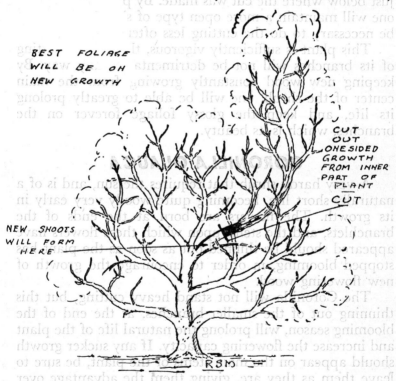

BEST FOLIAGE WILL BE ON NEW GROWTH

CUT OUT ONE SIDED GROWTH FROM INNER PART OF PLANT

CUT

NEW SHOOTS WILL FORM HERE

RSM

COPROSMA — SHOWING FRAMEWORK OF PLANT

and due to its natural rank habit of growth, requires considerable care in the way of pruning, to keep the plant at its best. Where allowed to grow year after year without any attention, it will become very open and unsightly. Old plants may be brought back to usefulness and beauty, regardless of their condition or lack of treatment in the past.

As this shrub is grown for its foliage only, it may be pruned at any time of the year, whenever a branch gets too far out of proportion, or the plant as a whole becomes too tall for the location in which it has been planted. When cutting out a branch, make the cut down in the body of the shrub, because the new growth will be formed just below where the cut was made. By pruning this way, one will maintain a more open type of shrub, and it will be necessary to do the cutting less often.

This plant is sufficiently vigorous, that severe cutting of its branches will not be detrimental in any way. By keeping new wood constantly growing from the main center of the shrub, one will be able to greatly prolong its life, and keep the glossy foliage forever on the branches, which is its beauty.

## CORONILLA GLAUCA

A very hardy shrub that requires the sun, and is of a naturally short life, becoming quite woody very early in its growth. The flowers are born at the ends of the branchlets, and the stems upon which these flowers have appeared should be thinned out as soon as the plant has stopped blooming, in order to encourage the growth of new flowering wood.

The Coronilla will not stand heavy cutting, but this thinning out of the smaller branches, at the end of the blooming season, will prolong the natural life of the plant and increase the flowering capacity. If any sucker growth should appear on the main stems of the plant, be sure to leave them as they are, giving them the advantage over any older wood. By the development of these suckers, the life of the plant may be greatly increased.

## CORREA, AUSTRALIAN FUCHSIA

Being a low spreading shrub, the Correas are liable to develop a sparce, open center if allowed to go un-pruned.

In order to avoid this unsightlyness a slight thinning ut should be done every year on the longest, most extended branches. This pruning should be done during the late fall, so that the flower buds will not be interrupted in their growth. Make these cuts almost to the base of the branches, leaving a short stub of three or four inches in length.

Pruning of any sort should not be needed until the plant is about four years old, and because of its growing habits, heavy thinning at one time should be avoided.

## COTONEASTER, *CRETAEGUS*
## (pannosa, franchetti, parnayi, simonsi, harrowviana, etc.)

Under this heading is included a very beautiful group of plants, and also ones that are most generously abused as to their proper care. By following a consistent system of cutting, such as is given below, your plants of this family may be kept practically the same size year after year, and loaded with berries every season.

The first thing to remember with this group, is that berries are borne on one year old wood only, and once that wood has produced a crop, it is through fruiting on that same wood. New wood must be produced each year for a proper setting of berries.

Pruning may start on the Cotoneasters any time after the plants are three years old, and should be done on all varieties, as soon as the bulk of the berries have fallen. In cutting sprays of berries for Christmas decoration, keep the pruning of the plant in mind. One full season of growth is required to produce wood upon which blossoms and fruit will appear. In other words, before a branch can set fruit, it must be one full year old, and at the time that branch is to be removed, it has passed

through two complete seasons. In cutting out these two
year old branches (the ones that have borne berries during the past summer and fall) cut them about six or eight
inches from their base. This will cause the new growth

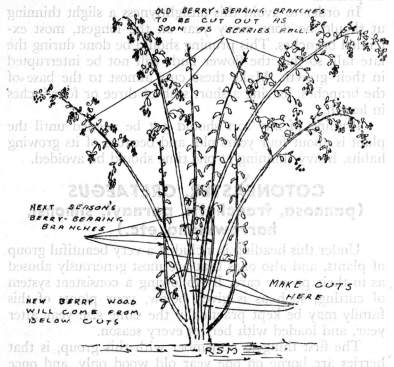

COTONEASTER — SHOWING FRUITING WOOD AND
NEXT SEASON'S FRUITING WOOD.

to push out on the old stub, within the first three or four
inches below the cut.

This family of plants is particularly subject to throwing out its new growth immediately below any major cut,
and this is the reason that they become top-heavy very
quickly when they are cut high, or hedged.

By following this system of removing the two year old
wood every year, after the plant is three years old, the
plant will always have plenty of new wood coming along
so that the heavy cutting will not denude the plant. Prac-

tically the entire growth in height is put on the branches during the first year, the second season being devoted to the development of berries. If these old branches are left on, they will send out small growths of fruit wood, but the number or size of the berries will not be as good as they could be if this system of pruning is carried on.

The smaller varieties of Cotoneaster require very little pruning. They being mostly of dwarf and trailing habits of growth, about the only thing that may be done with them is to keep them sufficiently thinned out, to encourage graceful growth. When making cuts on these plants, be sure to cut well down into the body of the plant, because the same rule holds, namely, the new growth will be concentrated just below where the cut was made.

## CUPRESSUS, CYPRESS

The Arizona and Monterey Cypress will not require any pruning whatever, but the Italian Cypress, the tall slender variety, will need some attention from time to time to keep it in proper shape.

Due to their tremendous popularity, the new plants could not be raised fast enough from properly selected cuttings, so they were grown in large quantities from seed that had been allowed to cross pollinate with other varieties and the result is now, that we have a great many supposedly Italian Cypress that are off type and never will be perfect specimens. Although, with good care these same plants can be made to look very much like perfect type trees.

When these Cypress trees begin to send out side branches that show a tendency to fall away from the main column of the plant, do not under any circumstances tie them back in place. This method merely prolongs the agony of a complete failure of the type of be desired. When these branches first start to pull away from the main column, cut off the end just a little inside of where it leaves the outside of the body of the tree (see illustration). This will cause lateral growth to shoot

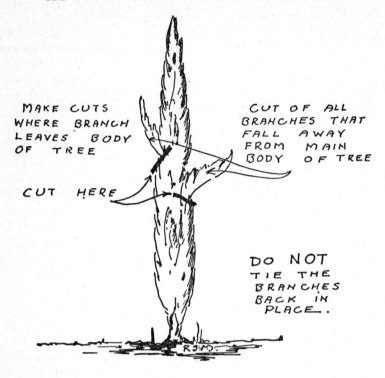

MAKE CUTS
WHERE BRANCH
LEAVES BODY
OF TREE

CUT OF ALL
BRANCHES THAT
FALL AWAY
FROM MAIN
BODY OF TREE

CUT HERE

DO NOT
TIE THE
BRANCHES
BACK IN
PLACE.

## ITALIAN CYPRESS

out below the cut and the hole that was made by the removal of the branch will soon be filled, and what is most important, the sturdiness of the plant will be greatly increased.

A light trimming of the outside tips will smooth up the general appearance, where the tree is used as a formal specimen.

## CYDONIA JAPONICA
## FLOWERING QUINCE

Pruning on this beautiful shrub should be done during the early winter, because as a result of a very mild season at this time of year, the plant may begin to throw out bloom very early in the spring, and any cutting should be done before the sap starts to flow.

The nature of the Cydonia seems to be to grow into a tangled mass of small limbs, and in order to preserve the main beauty of the plant these should be carefully thinned out, in order to open up the center of the shrub, making it possible to see the flowers that are borne on the inside. Select these branches to be thinned out from throughout the entire plant, so that the completed job will be one of even distribution in branches. The new growth around the outside should be headed back every winter, in order to throw the strength into the flowers. In doing this, only cut ofl about one-third of the branch that grew last summer, because the flowers will appear on the lower two-thirds. Bloom will appear on the same wood for several seasons, so it is not necessary to replenish the flowering wood every season, as it is with some shrubs.

## DEUTZIA, ALL VARIETIES

Like so many deciduous shrubs, the Deutzia will respond much better if more or less heavy pruning is carried on consistently every year. It will be noticed that after a branch has passed through three seasons' growth the amount of flowers borne will become less every year thereafter. If this old wood is removed, the plant will be kept with maximum bloom every season.

It is rather difficult to explain here just how to tell the age of these branches, where one is pruning their plant for the first time, but as this pruning should take place as soon as the blossoms fall, in the spring, it will be an easy thing to see which branches are to be removed.

Where this plant is to be pruned for the first time one may take out about one-quarter of the branches, or erect shoots, on the plant, selecting the largest ones. Cut these at their base, leaving a stub of about six or eight inches long, from which the new growth will develop. After this first year's pruning, it will be an easy matter to tell which are the older branches, the ones that have produced the least flowers.

## DIOSMA, BREATH OF HEAVEN

Because of the nature of this plant, being made up entirely of small, fine branchlets, there can be no heavy pruning done at any period of its life, except in the case of a very old plant which has never had any attention at all. In this case a general cutting back over the entire plant will sometimes cause it to come back with an abundance of new growth, and also, treatment of this kind will very often be such a severe shock as to kill the plant.

Where a plant is kept in good condition, year after year, it must be trimmed very lightly all over the outside of the plant, removing about two inches of tip growth over the entire plant. This should be done during January or early February, and the hedge shears are about as satisfactory an implement as any. The trimming that the plant receives under this method will cause it to put forth almost a solid mass of bloom, completely covering the outside of the shrub.

## DURANTA, GOLDEN DEWDROP

This is a very large growing shrub, but one that is always attractive when kept within its most beautiful dimensions. The golden berries that hang in such graceful clusters can be maintained much more abundantly when the plant has its correct trimming.

In treatment, it may be cared for in the same manner as the Cotoneasters. The flowers and berries are borne on branches that are one year old, so it is important to keep a supply of this type of growth coming on every year. The gracefully arching branches attain sufficient growth in one full season and next summer produce flowers followed by berries. These berries hang on the stems until late fall or winter, and before the spring growth starts, these berry producing branches should be cut down, leaving a short stub of from six to eight inches at the base, upon which the next crop of fruiting wood will be developed.

Like many other plants, new growth will be concentrated immediately below where a major cut has been made, so it is a decided mistake to trim these plants high. Such trimming will, in a very short time, develop a top-heavy shrub.

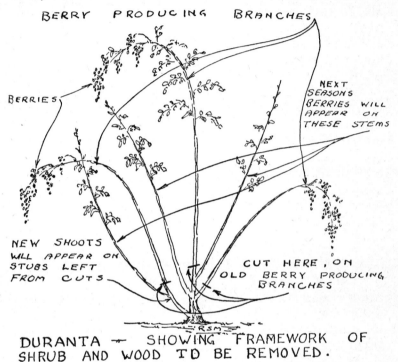

BERRY PRODUCING BRANCHES

BERRIES

NEXT SEASONS BERRIES WILL APPEAR ON THESE STEMS

NEW SHOOTS WILL APPEAR ON STUBS LEFT FROM CUTS

CUT HERE, ON OLD BERRY PRODUCING BRANCHES

DURANTA — SHOWING FRAMEWORK OF SHRUB AND WOOD TO BE REMOVED.

In case of frost-bitten branches, as often happens with this plant, cut just below the frosted area, which may be told by a loosening of the bark, throughout the frost bitten area.

## ELEAGNUS PUNGENS

This plant is one that would require pruning, according to the location in which it is planted. By nature it is of a very dense growth, of both spreading and upright habits, and is at its best when allowed to develop a mass of unrestricted foliage.

Where this shrub has been used in a location that requires restricted height, the plant may be kept very easily in control by selecting the taller branches, that are becoming obstructive, and cutting them out well down into the main body of the plant. This method will leave a "hole" for a time, but it will be quickly filled in with new growth. Treatment of this kind will also cause the lateral branches to send out new shoots.

The glossiness of the older leaves is very attractive, and a constant thinning out of the tip growth will maintain the heaviest foliage at all times. Pruning of this plant may be done at any time of the year, as it is grown primarily for its foliage.

## ERICA, HEATH OR HEATHER

The prostrate or trailing types of this plant will require no method of pruning, but the erect varieties, particularly the ones producing sufficient blooms to be of value as a house bouquet, will respond wonderfully to a good systematic cutting back each year. The Erica melanthera is possibly the most outstanding variety of this group.

These Heathers have a rather prolonged blooming period, and should be trimmed as soon as the majority of flowers have either withered or dropped. Depending upon the variety, the head of the flower spike may be from six inches to three feet in length, although the stem producing the spike may be somewhat longer. A cut should be made just below the main head of this bloom spike, which will leave a short stub of from a few inches to one foot in length. Upon this stub, the new wood will be formed, providing the blossom spikes for next season. By doing the pruning at the end of the flowering season, it will allow the plant sufficient time in which to develop new flowering wood for the next season.

Where the bloom is cut for decorative purposes, this method of pruning should be employed. In fact, if the

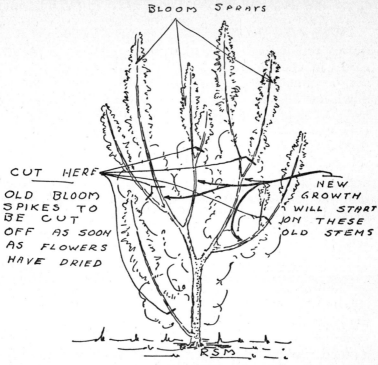

BLOOM SPRAYS

CUT HERE

OLD BLOOM
SPIKES TO
BE CUT
OFF AS SOON
AS FLOWERS
HAVE DRIED

NEW
GROWTH
WILL START
ON THESE
OLD STEMS

RSM

HEATHER — SHOWS CUTTING OF OLD
BLOOM SPRAYS

bloom is taken every year, the plant will be much improved.

It will be advisable not to remove any more of the old foliage than is absolutely needed in the pruning of the flower spikes, because this plant does not respond well to a too heavy shock by defoliating.

## ESCALLONIA

In this group of plants, are some very rank growing specimens, and will require a great deal of heavy cutting in order to keep them looking their best. The only one of this family, found commonly in this locality, not needing a great deal of pruning, is the E. Rubra, or the low growing red type. This variety will require a thinning out about every two years, and this cutting may be done during the winter months. In doing this, select the longest and oldest growths, cutting them out well down towards the base of the plant. New branches will take the place of those removed, in a short time.

The tall growing types will require very severe cutting back every winter, in order to keep them attractive. On the tall varieties, the old flowers and seed receptacles remain on the branches for a long time, and as new bloom will appear on fairly young wood, these old, large limbs that have borne flowers during the past season may be cut out. In making these cuts, try to even up the general shape of the shrub, as this plant has a tendency towards one-sidedness. These old branches may be cut down to within one foot of their base, allowing new shoots to be forced out. The more bushiness that can be developed in these plants the more beautiful will be the bloom.

## EUGENIA, MYRTIFOLIA, HOOKERI, and APICULATA, AUSTRALIAN BUSH CHERRY

The first named variety, E. myrtifolia, is one of the most beautiful tree-shrubs that can be grown when allowed to go absolutely untrimmed. Where this plant is used as a formal specimen or as a hedge, treat it the same as any other hedge growth. Where this type is used as a natural growth, some care should be exercised during the first few years of its development, in order to insure a substantial foundation for the tree to grow upon. This type should be staked, using an eight foot stake and the plant tied loosely to it. Do not tie too tight as this will cause unnatural weakening of the plant. See to it that the plant develops only one central stem. Many times, as a result of several possible causes, the terminal growth will divide, allowing two or more main stems to grow. If this occurs, pinch out all but the strongest. Allow all lateral growth, or side branches, to stay on,

44

up and down the trunk. When the plant attains a height of eight feet or more, it will usually take care of itself without any further training.

The E. Hookeri is one that will require small amounts of trimming two or three times a year, in order to keep it in good form, and the most possible foliage. Whether grown as a small tree or as a large shrub, the same system of trimming will apply. After the general desired shape has been established, all that will be needed from then

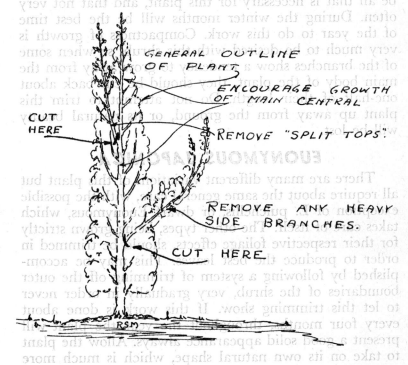

GENERAL OUTLINE OF PLANT.

ENCOURAGE GROWTH OF MAIN CENTRAL

CUT HERE

REMOVE "SPLIT TOPS".

REMOVE ANY HEAVY SIDE BRANCHES.

CUT HERE

RSM

EUGENIA MYRTIFOLIA — SHOWING DESIRABLE TYPE TO DEVELOP.

on, is to trim the outer edge of the twigs, in order to promote greater leaf growth. It would be better for this trimming to take place between the time the berries have ripened, and late spring, or it may be carried on through the flowering and fruiting period, providing that care is taken not to disturb any of the fruit producing wood.

The berries of this plant are not poisonous in any way, as so many people seem to believe; in fact the writer has eaten a rather good grade of jelly made from this fruit.

The E. apiculata, being a small growing shrub, entirely different from the other two types, requires an entirely different treatment. A light thinning out will be all that is necessary for this plant, and that not very often. During the winter months will be the best time of the year to do this work. Compactness of growth is very much to be desired with this shrub, so when some of the branches show a tendency to grow away from the main body of the plant, they should be cut back about one-half of their length. Do not attempt to trim this plant up away from the ground, or its natural beauty will be lost.

## EUONYMOUS JAPONICA

There are many different variations of this plant but all require about the same general care, with the possible exception of E. pulchellis, or dwarf Euonymous, which takes care of itself. The other types, being grown strictly for their respective foliage effects, should be trimmed in order to produce the best leaves. This may be accomplished by following a system of trimming off the outer boundaries of the shrub, very gradually in order never to let this trimming show. If this work is done about every four months, throughout the year the plant will present a good solid appearance always. Allow the plant to take on its own natural shape, which is much more attractive than any artificial form that the plant could be shaped into. In many localities on the Pacific coast, mildew is a considerable menace to all varieties of this plant family, and wherever it appears, it should be controlled as soon as possible with some good fungicidal spray.

As this plant is, in most localities, a rank grower, it

is advisable to carry on a constant system of trimming, rather than have to resort to heavy pruning every three or four years, as this sort of treatment would result in coarse unsightly growth.

## FABIANA IMBRICATA

This is a fast growing shrub that soon becomes unsightly with lack of care, but may be kept very attractive indefinitely with one proper pruning a year. The long spikes of bloom are borne on branches that have attained one full season's growth, and these branches should be removed as soon as the flowers have passed. Do not hesitate to cut this shrub heavily, as it seems to thrive on treatment of this sort.

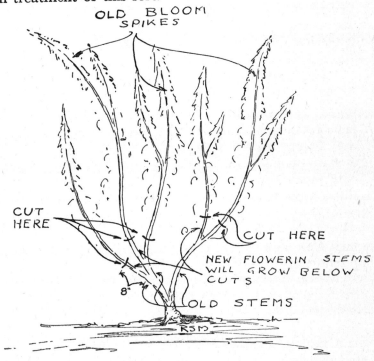

FABIANA — SHOWING METHOD OF PRODUCING MORE AND BETTER FLOWERING WOOD.

This plant blossoms usually in May and June, and as soon as the flowers are finished, the entire bloom spike should be cut back, leaving a short stub at the base about six or eight inches in length. The next season's flowering wood will spring from these stubs, and will have ample time between the pruning and next flowering season, to produce another fine crop of bloom spikes. Where this system is carried out very year, the shrub will simply be loaded with flowers at the proper time, and will always be a shrub of beauty, instead of a disfigurement, as is so often the case where this plant is neglected.

These long sprays of bloom combine well as a large bouquet, and where they are to be cut during full bloom, this system of pruning should be adhered to. In fact, taking the blossoms at their height, will allow the plant just so much more time in which to produce next season's flowering wood.

## FATSIA JAPONICA (Aralia Sieboldi)

Very little can be done in any way of pruning on this plant, except in the case of old specimens, where they have become too tall for their location. In this case they may be cut back during the late Spring, and as they are a plant inclined to developing just one main stem, the only way to do it is to cut the main stem off at about a three foot height from the ground. Unfortunately this will sometimes cause the plant to die, but where this cutting is done in late Spring, the chances are very favorable that it will recover. Where a small shoot has started out from the base, there will be little or no danger of losing the plant, as a result of this heavy cutting. A new top will be developed as a result of this heavy heading.

## FLOWERING PEACHES

There is no flowering tree that is any more beautiful in the Spring, and if more people realized that by heavy cutting they could produce more and finer blooms on their Flowering Peaches, they would not hesitate to give them the pruning that is needed.

In Southern California particularly these trees are apt only to live half their possible lives as a result of neglecting to cut. Pruning should start as soon as the plant has put out its first crop of bloom, and be done every year thereafter. As soon as the flower petals have fallen is the proper time to do this cutting back, and remember that you are actually doing the tree a favor when you cut severely.

The Flowering Peach will bear flowers on wood that has had one complete season's growth, and as soon as this wood has produced its crop, it should be cut back to allow new flowering wood to replace it. In the Spring, when this cutting is done, the sap is very active, and

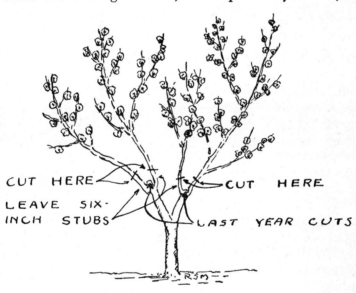

CUT HERE
LEAVE SIX-
INCH STUBS
CUT HERE
LAST YEAR CUTS

FLOWERING PEACH — MAKE
CUTS AS SOON AS PETALS HAVE
FALLEN IN SPRING — REMOVE ALL
THE OLD FLOWERIN WOOD.

although there may be some exuding of gum, on the bark, there is little danger of sour-sap harming the tree.

As soon as the petals have fallen, cut out all of the past season's growth, leaving short stubs of from four to six inches long at their base. The new flowering wood will spring from these stubs in a very short time and will have ample time in which to develop for next season's flowers.

This system will not only produce more and larger individual flowers, but will also almost double the life of the tree. The Peach, being a rather weak wood, is prone to develop internal rot when growing slow, and this system of pruning will very materially lessen the possibility of the tree being weakened from this disease, due to the fact that the tree is kept in vigorous growth all of the time.

## FORSYTHIA VIRRIDISSIMA
## GOLDEN BELL

This shrub should be pruned each year after it is three years old, in order to prevent its growing too rank. As the growth on the Forsythia is extremely fast, the plant will grow all out of bounds if not properly cared for, and this means heavy pruning.

The long arching branches that have attained two seasons of growth should be cut out, and this work should be done as soon as the plant has stopped growing in early winter. It will be noticed that the best flowers will appear in the second year's growth, so after this best bloom has been produced let the plant develop new wood by cutting out the old branches.

The branches that are to be cut out should be cut almost to their base, leaving about an eight-inch stub on which the new shoots will develop the following spring. By keeping the plant cut back under the above system, it will be a shrub of much greater beauty and a real ornament to one's yard.

Do not attempt to tie this plant up to a stake. It is

by nature a spreading habit of growth, and any attempt to force it away from this habit will destroy the main attraciveness of the plant.

## FUCHSIAS

Although there are a great many varieties of Fuchsia that are popular in our gardens, the habits of growth are near enough alike, so that one method of cutting back will apply to all. There are two system of pruning that may be done on these plants with equal results in the end.

The first system, which would be the most ideal from the standpoint that the plant would be kept in bloom more constantly, is to do necessary cutting throughout the entire year, about every four months, and keep the wood that has grown too tall, thinned out, also to remove any twigs that show signs of becoming leafless. In making these cuts, take the branches out well down into the center of the plant, always keeping in mind to get as near perfect balance in the outer dimensions of the plant as possible.

The second system is one of severe cutting, and the most advantageous time to do this cutting is during January. This severe cutting should not be needed more than every two years. Select a well distributed framework of the older branches, about one-third of the total height of the shrub, and cut practically all of the heaviest branches down to this framework. The following heavy cuttings should always be cut back to this frame, but leaving short stubs at the base of the wood that is being cut back. These stubs should be about three inches long.

These heavy prunings will remove practically all of the foliage, and some bloom, but the plant will recover quickly, and better flowers will appear on this new wood.

## GARDENIA, CAPE JASMINE

The Gardenia is a rather slow growing plant, and will require very little in the way of pruning, except a very slight thinning out, and this is usually done when the

51

bloom is picked. They are by nature a very even growing plant, but should one become unbalanced in growth, it may be overcome easily by trimming off any growth that is forcing the plant into one-sidedness.

The plants seem to produce best when kept at about a thirty inch height, and when they attempt to get taller than this, the tall growth should be cut back to the main body of the plant.

## GENISTA (cytissus) Broom

Under this heading is included a family of plants very much planted, and possibly about as much neglected as any group that are used. They all being rapid growers, are very apt to get out of bounds early in life, so in order

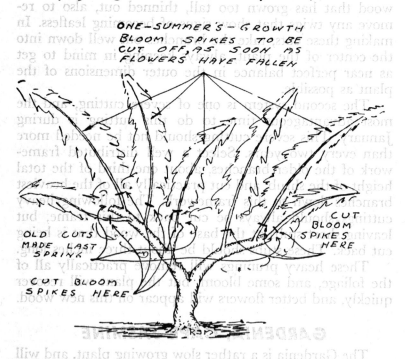

ONE-SUMMER'S-GROWTH
BLOOM SPIKES TO BE
CUT OFF, AS SOON AS
FLOWERS HAVE FALLEN

CUT
BLOOM
SPIKES
HERE

OLD CUTS
MADE LAST
SPRING

CUT BLOOM
SPIKES HERE

GENISTA FRAGRANS — RACEMOSA — SHOWING
ANNUAL CUTTING OF BLOOM SPIKES.

to preserve the beauty of the plant they should be pruned severly every year according to the following system:

The Genista or Cytissus, fragans, racemosus, and canariensis will all respond to this method. Flowers are produced upon wood that has had one full season's growth and when this wood has put forth one crop of bloom, it should be removed and allowed to develop new flowering wood for next year. These varieties should have these old bloom bearing branches cut out almost completely, leaving a short stub of about four inches at the base, from which the new growth will develop. Do not remove any other fine secondary growth, as these small branches will have sufficient leaves to keep the sap of the plant active until the new shoots start. Make these heavy cuts as soon as the flowers have fallen in the Spring.

Where one has an old plant that has never received any particular system of pruning, simply stub the entire plant off at about thirty inches from the ground, as soon as it is through blooming, and follow the above specified method every year after this. The writer has developed bloom bearing branches four and five feet in length every year with this method, and also kept the plant at about the same size for many years.

Another variety very greatly used, is the Genista juncea, or Spanish Broom, a very free blooming type that only requires attention about every three years, and then of a rather severe nature. Whenever the plant has attaind too much height for its location, or is running rather shy of bloom due to its increased size, it may be treated in this manner: Select about one-half of the main stems throughout the plant and remove them with a pruning saw at from two to three feet from the ground. This will cause new growth to force out over the entire plant. The following year take out the old stems that were left from the first pruning. This work may be done in the late summer to best advantage.

The white flowering types of Genista, and the Scotch Broom, will respond best to a thinning out of the old flower producing wood as soon as the bloom is past. In removing this wood, cut deep into the body of the plant in order to promote the growth of inside branches.

## GREVILLEA BANKSI and THELEMANNIANA

Heavy pruning on either one of these two plants will act as more of a detriment than a benefit. They are both naturally rather compact in growth, and never require any cutting, for the good of the plant.

Frequently though, the plant is set out in a location where it cannot attain its full height without interfering with some other object, and in this case they may be reduced in height by thinning out the uppermost of the interfering branches. When doing this cutting, remove the wood well down into the body of the plant. The late spring will be the most advantageous time of year to perform this pruning.

If cutting any of the flowers for bouquets, it would be best to select the branchlets from the thickest portions of foliage, and not too many from one spot, because this plant is very slow in recovering from cutting of any sort.

## HAKEA

This family comprises a very hardy, slow growing group that will require practically nothing in the way of pruning. About the only place that cutting back will be required is when the shrub attains too great a height for location in which it is planted. When this does become necessary, remove whatever limbs are interfering and cut them well down into the body of the plant. This work may be done at any time of the year. This type of plant does not respond well to outside trimming, or hedging.

## HEDGES

The treatment required in the trimming of any hedge is possibly the simplest form of pruning, and yet this sort of work may be greatly simplified with the use of a line or string with which to assist in one's efforts. The human eye is not always infallible, and so in this case should be aided by the employment of a tightly stretched string.

The writer has always found it easier to trim off the top of the hedge first. By stretching a line from one end of the hedge to the other, a little to the side, but at the same level that the newly trimmed top is to be, and trimming with the shears down to the level of this line, one will be assured of a perfectly even top. (See illustration.)

Next, by setting stakes at either end of the hedge, in line with the new side of the hedge, and stretching a line along the top, and one along the ground if possible, then trimming out all growth outside an alignment between the two strings, the result will be a very neat appearance the first time over.

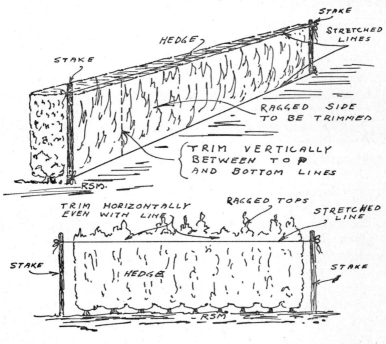

HEDGE TRIMMING — SHOWING METHOD OF TRIMMING TO STRETCHED-LINES

With some hedges, it will be necessary to give a heavy trimming once a year, and the best time to do this is in the spring, just before the new buds begin to develop for the summer's growth. If at this time, a good accurate job is done, the balance of the lighter trimming may be done as often as necessary during the summer without the aid of the side or top guiding lines. The more often the hedge is trimmed, the more dense will be the foliage.

In starting a new hedge, it is advisable to allow the new plants to attain their full height, or that is, the height that is desired of the hedge, before stopping the terminal or end growth. Once this height is attained, never allow any growth to go above it. As the plants grow from this point on they will fill in the body of the hedge, creating the good solid effect for which it was planted.

## HIBISCUS

Up to the time that these plants are five years old or more they require little in the way of pruning, but as they get older the main body of the plant will lose its compactness and cutting will have to be done in order to restore the beauty of the shrub.

The Hibiscus should not be cut heavily at any one time. Being of an open type of growth, it will be noticed when the plant is getting too large for its location, that the larger branches have a tendency to grow out from the general center of the plant, at all angles. In selecting wood to be cut out, pick the limbs from several parts of the plant, so that too big a hole is not left in any one place. Don't remove more than one-third of the largest branches at any one time, and it will be better to allow about three or four months to elapse between heavy cuttings. These larger branches should be cut back about two-thirds of their total length, which will cause new twigs to start over the entire plant. This will spread the heavier pruning through almost one year, but the plant will respond more satisfactorily than though it had all been done at once.

56

With the Hibiscus, the best flowers are produced when the plant is growing rapidly, and this cutting out of the old coarse wood will promote this better than any

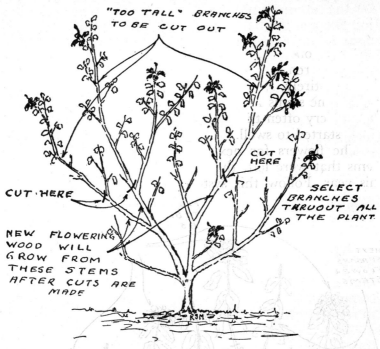

HIBISCUS — SHOWING METHOD OF THINNING OUT BRANCHES

thing else that can be done. Where all the wood is left on these plants, year after year, the flowers will gradually lessen in size until they are about one-half normal.

## HYDRANGEA

This beautiful flowering shrub is one that is liked by almost everyone, and yet is understood by very few, as to the proper care needed to produce the largest flowers. Fortunately though, it will produce some flowers under extreme neglect.

It will be noticed that when the plant is in full bloom,

only about one-half of the stems have produced flower heads, which is a perfectly natural condition. The stems that did not produce flowers this season are the ones that will have the bloom next year. When the flowers have dried up or fallen, every one of the stems upon which the flower heads were borne should be removed. This is important if one would have nothing but the finest quality bloom. In removing these stems, they should be cut out almost entirely, leaving only two buds or leaf scars at the base of the stems from which future flowering wood will come. Very often these buds that are to be left have already started to swell.

The flowers for next season will appear upon the stems that were left, the ones that were without bloom this year. Follow this system every year, removing all

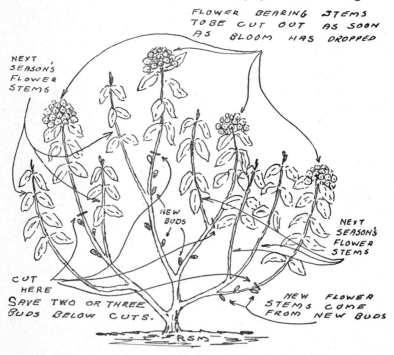

HYDRANGEA — SHOWING THREE STAGES OF FLOWER STEM DEVELOPMENT.

stems that bore flowers, and this work should be done as soon as the flowers have withered.

Pruning should not start before a plant is four years old, and should be done every year thereafter.

# HYPERICUM, GOLD FLOWER
## (Upright Types)

This is a very free blooming plant when kept in good condition, but can become unattractive quickly when not given the proper attention. It should be pruned in the late fall or early winter. The best flowers are borne on young wood, so this type of growth should be forced along every year.

No branch of this plant should be allowed to stay on the plant for more than three seasons, and with some varieties, according to location, two summers will be enough. By selecting the oldest wood, or that which is lacking in foliage, and cutting it out entirely, leaving about a four inch stub at the base, upon which new wood will develop, the plant will maintain graceful proportions and have ever so much more bloom upon it than where it were allowed to grow unhampered.

The Hypericum floribunda, a very free flowering type, grows very fast, and the flower bearing wood should not be allowed to remain on the plant for more than two seasons for the best results.

All of this family will give more flowers when not allowed to be kept too wet. An abundance of moisture will cause them to run to foliage rather than bloom.

# IOCHROMA

Both the red and blue varieties of the plant are almost identical as to habits of growth and care. They are fast growers and should receive a heavy pruning every year after they are past their second summer. The best flowers are borne on the new wood, as well as the leaves being more luxuriant on this type of growth.

The suckers that will spring up from the bottom as

a result of heavy cutting, will produce the finest quality of flowers, so everything should be done to encourage these shoots. The proper time of year for pruning to be done on this plant is in the spring, after the cold weather has passed. When the tall upright stems have reached a height of six feet or more, and are beginning to be shy of leaves along the lower portions, the entire stem should be cut out, almost to the ground, leaving a short stub of from six to eight inches. The new suckers will sprout from this area. Refrain from tying the branches of this plant if possible. The new growth should and will support its own weight when given the opportunity. Tying disfigures the beauty of this shrub considerably.

## ITEA, ILICIFOLIA, AND YUNNANENSIS — SWEET SPIRE

These two varieties are usually planted for use as screening plants, because of their dense foliage and abundant growth. Therefore, the only pruning that will be necessary will be the removal of any old branches that have become too old and leafless, or are too low on the shrub to be of any value for screen purposes. Cutting should be done during the winter months.

When branches are to be cut out, they should be removed at their base, never high on the branch, because like the Pyrachanthas, or Cotoneasters, new growth will concentrate itself immediately below where a cut was made. High cutting or "hedging" of this plant will develop a top-heavy shrub very soon, causing an uncontrollable habit of growth, as well as sparse foliage low down in the body of the plant.

As these shrubs grow, they continually put up a considerable number of tall growing branches, which gradually arch over, making a graceful, spreading appearance. As these branches are slowly pushed to the outer borders of the plant, they finally are very close to the ground, and become shy of leaves from lack of sunlight. These lowering branches should be cut out, clear to their

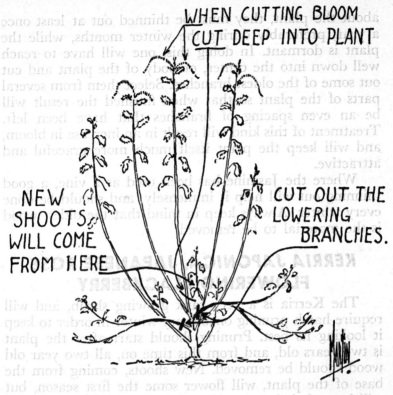

WHEN CUTTING BLOOM
CUT DEEP INTO PLANT

NEW SHOOTS WILL COME FROM HERE

CUT OUT THE LOWERING BRANCHES.

## ITEA. OR SWEETSPIRE.

base, which will force new, erect branches to replace them in the center of the shrub.

If the fragrant bloom tassels are to be used for house decorations, try to follow this system of pruning, for the benefit of the plant.

## JASMINE

This group of plants is ordinarily used as vines but some types will grow into very creditable shrubs if treated as such under the correct method of pruning. By nature all of the Jasmines are rather a rank wild growth, and in order to maintain any degree of graceful order about the plant, they must be thinned out at least once a year, preferably during the winter months, while the plant is dormant. In doing this, one will have to reach well down into the center, or body of the plant and cut out some of the oldest branches. Select them from several parts of the plant so that when finished the result will be an even spacing of branches that have been left. Treatment of this kind will result in an increase in bloom, and will keep the plant itself much more graceful and attractive.

Where the Jasmine has been used as a vine, a good thinning out will help it immensely, and should be done every winter. Always keep in mind that the oldest wood is the material to be removed.

## KERRIA JAPONICA, JAPANESE ROSE FLOWERING BLACKBERRY

The Kerria is a very rank growing shrub, and will require harsh pruning once every winter in order to keep it looking its best. Pruning should start after the plant is two years old, and from this time on, all two year old wood should be removed. New shoots, coming from the base of the plant, will flower some the first season, but will have their heaviest bloom the second summer. After this second season, these arching branches should be cut down almost to the ground, which will force new shoots to come up to replace them.

In the case of an old plant that has never received a proper cutting back, thin out all of the old coarse stems, cutting them clear to the ground, leaving enough of the younger shoots to be about one-half of the top growth.

Old clumps of this plant will show a tendency to spreading, by the throwing out of root-suckers. Many of these should be removed, by digging down with a spade, and cutting them off. The plant will do just as well by being confined in a small area.

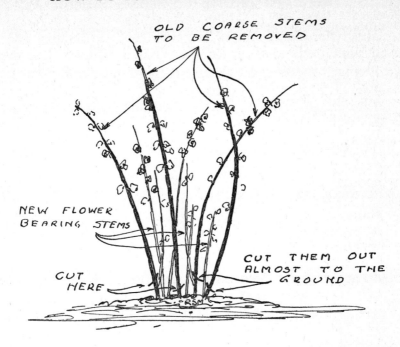

KERRIA — SHOWING METHOD OF
THINNING OUT

## LAGERSTROEMIA INDICA
## CREPE MYRTLE

This tree-shrub will need but very little attention as far as pruning is concerned. By nature it is very slow growing, and as the bloom is borne at the tips of the branches, there is no way in which pruning will increase the amount of flowers. Too much water will have a tendency to make the plant bloom less, the growth all going into foliage and wood. It is by nature a very drought resisting plant.

In some cases the branches of the Crepe Myrtle may crowd somewhat, and if such a thing does happen they should be thinned out to allow good open growth. Permitting good open growth in this plant will assure maximum bloom. Thin out the branches so that each one stands out individually. Any crossing or interfering wood should be cut out.

This plant is a very decided sun lover, and will not respond well when grown in the shade. An indication of too much shade is a presence of mildew on the leaves and being shy on bloom during the flowering season. Where this condition arises, the plant should either be moved to a new sunny location during the winter months, or whatever it is shutting out the sunlight, should be removed where it is possible to do so.

## LANTANA

This is a plant that will require little pruning, as it is one of rough, compact habits of growth. However, there are always old plants that have grown beyond their reasonable limits of beauty, and should be brought back to a smaller proportion. In the late spring the Lantana may be given a very severe cutting back without hurting it in the least. To do this, simply cut away every branch down to the desired height, and in a very short time new growth will appear and the plant will be in full bloom again.

When this dehorning has been finished it is a good plan to remove any branches that have a tendency to interfere with each other, and will make the new growth more even in distribution.

Another method, that will take great patience, but one that will preserve more of the beauty of the plant during its period of being changed from one size to the other, is to follow a consistent method of thinning out the branches, selecting the longest ones first. Take out a few branches every two months, until the plant is back down to a desired size. In cutting out these branches, cut them well down into the main body of the plant. This latter system can be done at any time of the year, but the heaviest cutting should be done in the spring.

## LAUROCERASUS OFFICINALLIS, ENGLISH LAUREL

This beautiful shrub, when allowed to grow naturally, attains very attractive proportions, or it may be kept at about a six foot height indefinitely, with good foliage, where one takes the proper care of it.

It is a mistake to trim this plant around the outside, hedge fashion, because in doing this one loses the effectiveness of its luxuriant foliage. By thinning out the branches when they become too tall, new shoots will be kept growing in the inner part of the plant as a result of the cutting. In cutting out these taller branches select them throughout the entire plant, so that their removal will not be noticeable; cut them well down into the body of the shrub, leaving a short stub at the base, of about four inches.

Where it is wanted that the plant should be more spreading, the topmost shoots should be thinned out, but do not trim off the top entirely as this would create an artificial appearance.

Pruning on this plant should be done in the early spring, before any major growth has commenced. One pruning a year should be sufficient.

## LEONOTUS LEONORUS, LION'S TAIL

Under most conditions, this is a very fast growing shrub, and one that will require severe cutting, in order to prolong the flowering period. By proper pruning the blooming can be stretched out to last two or three times as long as is normal.

Pruning may begin any time after the shrub is two years old or more, but regardless of age, treat the plant to this same system of care. This plant will bear flowers on wood that has grown for a few months, and once the bloom has gone, that stem will be rather unsightly if allowed to stay on the plant. By following a system of rotation, and doing the necessary pruning every four months throughout the year, each time cutting out one-

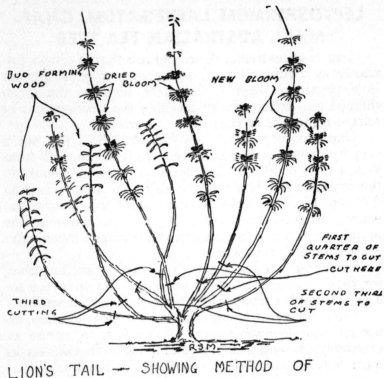

BUD FORMING WOOD

DRIED BLOOM

NEW BLOOM

FIRST QUARTER OF STEMS TO CUT

CUT HERE

SECOND THIRD OF STEMS TO CUT

THIRD CUTTING

RSM

LION'S TAIL — SHOWING METHOD OF ROTATING FLOWERING WOOD

third of the oldest flower bearing stems, the blooming period will be greatly lengthened. The first time that this pruning is attended to, select about one-third of the erect stems, those that now have the old dried seed receptacles at each joint, and cut them almost to the ground, leaving a stub of from six to seven inches, from which the new growth will start. At the end of four months remove half of the remaining old stems in like manner, and four months later remove the balance of the old stems. By this time there will be plenty of new wood formed and during the next summer one will notice the considerably longer flowering period. This system of pruning may be carried on year after year, to the betterment of the shrub.

## LEPTOSPERMUM LAEVEGATUM, CHAP-MANI, AUSTRALIAN TEA TREE

This is an extremely hardy shrub that is grown primarily as a foliage plant, and therefore requiring but little pruning, except to keep the body of the shrub thinned out sufficiently to promote the development of foliage on the inner part of the plant.

Under natural conditions this plant will put out a very heavy mat of fine branches which in time will form such a mass of foliage that the light cannot penetrate to the center of the plant, thus causing the inner leaves to die out. If about once a year, preferably during the winter, a good proportion of the last season's fine branches are removed, the plant will retain a much more graceful habit of growth.

Encourage the development of the arching branches, for these, as time goes on, will form the structure for a very beautiful shrub with the former named variety.

After this plant is established in its new location, do not let it have much water, because it is by nature an extremely drought resistant plant, and will take on its more natural proportions when kept fairly dry.

## LIGUSTRUM, PRIVET

Within this group of shrubs are extremely hardy and in the majority of cases very fast growers, that are usually planted to obtain a quick screen effect. After the screen effect has been attained, it is sometimes desirable not to have the plants grow above that height, and where it is not wanted to have a formal hedge effect, the desired height may be maintained indefinitely by keeping the plants thinned out, or removing some of the largest, coarsest branches every year. Because of the rapid growth of these plants, this treatment will not hurt them, and will also tend to keep the plants of a more graceful proportion.

In doing this thinning out, select the branches that are the largest, or growing most out of bounds. Take them out entirely, well down into the body of the plant. Remove sufficient of these branches to bring the plant back to the desired height. These plants, like so many others, will concentrate their new growth just below a major cut, so this system will develop growth down in the center of the plant where it will do the most good.

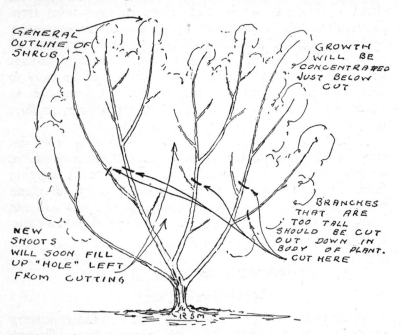

LIGUSTRUM OR PRIVET — SHOWING METHOD OF CUTTING WHEN USED AS A SPECIMEN OR INDIVIDUAL SHRUB.

As the Privets are grown mainly as a foliage plant, the pruning may be done at any time of the year, but the heaviest cutting should be done during the winter while the plant is dormant.

## LILAC, EASTERN AND PERSIAN

The Pacific coast, particularly the southern portion, does not seem to be the best place in which to grow the

Eastern Lilac. However, in places where the winters are quite cold, it will flower very well. The plant seems to require a cold winter to force it into dormancy. Even in Southern California, the Lilac will do better if allowed to become absolutely dormant during the winter, and this condition may be brought about by not allowing the shrub to get any water aside from natural rains from September first on. A dry condition such as suggested, will cause all of the leaves to drop, and therefore all growth will be suspended until spring. Larger flowers will follow a complete rest period. This applies only to such localities where the winters are mild enough to allow the plant to grow all through the winter, as they will do if given the opportunity.

The Lilac is very much given to suckering from the roots, and these suckers should be cut off smooth as soon as they appear. This should be done by digging down below ground level, and cutting them off clean where they leave the root. Pruning off the top will not be necessary. The development of suckers should be discouraged as much as possible.

## LONICERA NITIDA, BLACK HONEYSUCKLE

Although this is of the Honeysuckle family, it very rarely blooms in this locality, and is planted as a foliage plant entirely, sometimes being used as a hedge.

When used as a specimen plant, the appearance may be greatly improved by keeping the older branches thinned out from the body of the plant. After the upright, slightly arching branches have become three years old or more they are inclined to lose their leaves and become very ragged in appearance. These branches should be removed to allow new growth and give the shrub a fresher appearance. Cut these branches out almost to the ground, by following them down to their base. This work can be done more easily with a knife, and may be done during the winter months.

The beauty of the plant is in the very dark glossy green new leaves, and the above mentioned system of pruning will keep the new leaves coming along all the time. Old foliage soon becomes dull.

## MAGNOLIA, SHRUB VARIETIES, SOLANGEANA, KOBUS STELLATA, LILIFLORA, ETC.

This group of Magnolias will require very little in the way of pruning, because by habit, they shape themselves, and any systematic pruning will not necessarily improve the amount or quality of bloom.

During the early winter months, while the plants are bare of leaves, any interfering branches may be cut out, in such a way as to leave an even branch distribution throughout the plant. In making these cuts, remove an undesirable branch as low down on the main stem as will be necessary to even up the branch arrangement.

Young plants may be made to grow more stockily during their first few years by pinching out the tip buds of the upright branches during their growing period in summer. This treatment will force lateral growth up and down these same branches and make a more heavily branched shrub.

## MAHONIA AQUIFOLIA, OREGON HOLLY-GRAPE, AND OTHER MAHONIAS

During the early years of this plant's life, it will require no pruning of any kind, as the natural irregularity of growth gives it charm. After the shrub is four or five years old, though, it will be best to prune out some of the oldest, coarsest upright branches, in order to develop new sucker growth. In about one season, this type of wood will begin to fill in the lower portion of the shrub, with new leaves, flowers and berries.

In making cuts of this sort, select the oldest and roughest appearing stems that have either grown too tall and straggling, or are becoming too unsightly in other ways, and cut them out about ten inches from the ground. Try to arrange this cutting, so that not more than two or three of these branches are removed at a time,

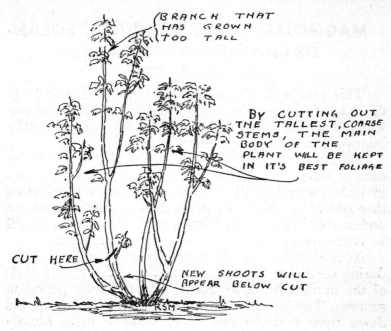

BRANCH THAT HAS GROWN TOO TALL

BY CUTTING OUT THE TALLEST, COARSE STEMS, THE MAIN BODY OF THE PLANT WILL BE KEPT IN IT'S BEST FOLIAGE

CUT HERE

NEW SHOOTS WILL APPEAR BELOW CUT

MAHONIA — OREGON HOLLY-GRAPE — SHOWING SYSTEM TO THIN OUT STEMS.

as the plant does not respond very well to severe pruning. The best time of the year to do this pruning will be in the late spring.

Never trim this shrub along the top of the plant, as this sort of treatment will not aid in the appearance in any way.

## MELALEUCA, BOTTLE BRUSH

In this group are included a considerable assortment of plants, but they will respond to the same system of pruning. It is their nature to develop a mass of fine branches, and where a large specimen is wanted it will be necessary to thin out some of these to properly shape the plant. If greater density is wanted, this may be brought about by trimming off the tips of the branches on the sides and top of the plant. Where the plant is growing too tall for the location in which it has been planted, do not trim off the top only, as one might a hedge, but thin out the tallest branches, cutting them well down into the body of the shrub. Do not leave a stub, as this sort of plant does not sucker readily from old wood.

Pruning should be done after the blooming season has passed. These plants will bloom more profusely if allowed to go quite dry.

## MYRTUS COMMUNIS, ETC., ENGLISH MYRTLE

Although there are many varieties of this plant found commonly among our gardens, one system of pruning will apply to all equally well. This family of plants is also used a great deal for hedging, and in this use, treat the same as any other hedge. Where allowed to grow in its natural form, it will always be a very attractive plant.

Where a natural growth is desired, the outside tip growth should never be trimmed back, as this will merely form a solid exterior, and the charm of its slight irregularity will be lost. As the plant grows, there will be occasions when it may become too tall for the location in which it has been planted, and at this time a careful thinning out should be done. Select the taller branches evenly spaced throughout the plant, and cut them out, reaching well down into the main body of the plant.

Frequently a plant will become too heavy on one side due to too rapid growth. This may also be controlled by pruning. Cut out the branches on the under side of the part that has receded from the rest of the plant, and this will cause new growth to start which will soon fill up the gap left by the pulling away of one side. Never tie up a plant in this condition, even though it may remedy the disfigurement quickly, because tying will remove all natural strength, causing the branches ever afterward to be weak and unable to support their own weight.

Pruning should be done during the winter.

The dwarf varieties will not require pruning of any kind.

## NANDINA DOMESTICA
## SACRED BAMBOO

Like the Hollygrape, this plant will not require any pruning the early years of its life, and will only need

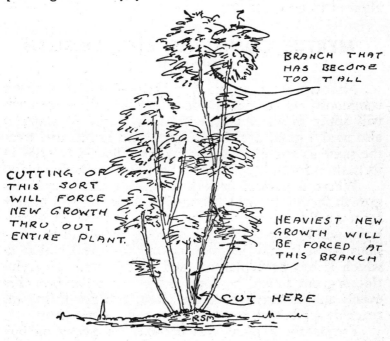

NANDINA — SHOWING HOW STEMS
SHOULD BE THINNED OUT —

attention when it becomes too tall for the location in which it has been planted.

When treatment becomes necessary, one should remember that sucker growth should be encouraged from the base of the plant. This is accomplished by cutting out the stems that are getting too tall, or that are becoming unsightly due to the lack of foliage. Cut these stems down to about ten inches of the ground. On this plant new shoots will not start immediately as a result of severe cutting, but with treatment of this sort, these new shoots will start in good time. The best time of year to do this cutting will be in the early spring, after the color of the foliage has turned back to green again. By pruning the plant when it is dormant, during the winter, one will lose the brilliant coloring that appears during cold weather.

## NERIUM OLEANDER, OLEANDER

This shrub is used about equally as a tree and as a shrub, and for each case, an exactly opposite system of pruning is recommended.

When used as a tree, the young plant should be staked for the first three or four years, using material two inches square, or iron pipe. Allow no shoots to develop on the stem but the terminal growth, or that is, pinch off any buds that form anywhere along the stem but at the end. Keep this up until the tip has reached a six foot height, then the top will take care of itself. Perhaps a little thinning will be needed in order to insure a perfectly balanced top. Suckers will appear from time to time at the base and these should not be cut off, but *pulled*. Dig down below the surface to where the suckers start from the root stock, and pull them off. The reason for this is that in pulling, all of the bud tissue will come away with the sucker, while if a cut were made other suckers would reappear in a short time. This will not eliminate the growth of additional suckers, but it will greatly retard them.

In tying the stem to the stake, be sure that the tying is very loose; just enough to act as a guide, not a support. Tight tying causes the stem to develop no strength of its own.

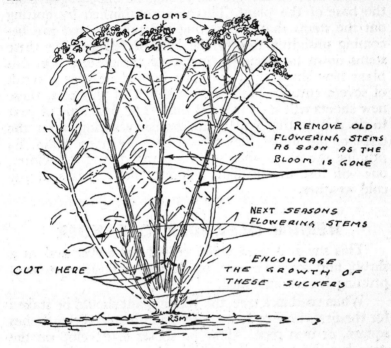

OLEANDER — SHOWING METHOD OF PRUNING WHEN USED AS A SHRUB.

Where a tree of lower head is desired, let the top care for itself as soon as the tip has reached the desired height. The same treatment as above will apply from then on.

Where this plant is to be used as a shrub the sucker growth is encouraged, in order to keep the plant at about an even height and constantly replenish the flowering wood. As soon as a bloom cluster has finished flowering, the entire stem should be removed by cutting it out almost to the ground, which will cause a new growth to replace it. Pruning should not be started on Oleanders until they are at least four years old. Nothing will be needed up until this age. This same treatment can be applied to old plants that have never been pruned before, although it may take some two or three years to get the plant back into good shape where it has been neglected for too long a time.

## PHILADELPHUS, SYRINGA, MOCK ORANGE

One system of pruning will apply to all of the shrubby Philadelphus. The vining type may be treated as any other vine should be.

This plant is one that will take on very large proportions if uncared for, but one can keep it much more attractive by not allowing it to grow more than about six feet in height. As the older shoots reach a height above this, they should be taken out to allow the new growth to take their place. The younger wood will bear the most prolific bloom.

This pruning can be done during the winter months but if one will wait until the flowers have fallen in the spring there will still be ample time in which to do the cutting. As soon as the shrub has put out its spring bloom cut out these oldest upright stems down to their base, leaving a stub of about one foot length. New shoots will form upon these which will produce several seasons of flowers before it will be necessary for them to be removed in their turn.

By keeping the height of the Philadelphus down to within six feet, there will always be good foliage and bloom on the lower portion, which is inclined to become quite bare when allowed to grow uncut. Sprays of bloom may be cut from the smaller wood without harming the plant in any way.

This is another shrub whose flowering ability will be greatly improved if allowed to go quite dry after the first of September. This treatment will force the plant to stop all branch growth, with the result that the bloom will be much finer the next spring.

## PHOTINIA ARBUTIFOLIA and SERRULATA
## CALIFORNIA HOLLY

All that would be advisable in the way of pruning for this hardy native is to remove only that wood which has a tendency to overbalance the plant. Under cultivated conditions the Holly is very apt to take a most irregular habit of growth, and this should be corrected from time to time very sparingly. The best berry clusters will be borne on the ends of newly produced branches, so do not trim off any tip growth unless absolutely necessary. Where any branches are too high for its location, or growing too one-sided, thin these branches out by cutting them well down into the main body of the plant. Do not leave stubs at the base of a branch.

The proper time of year to do any cutting is the winter, when the berries have all disappeared. As the fruit bearing wood takes several seasons to produce, the less cutting that is done the better the berry crop will be. Keep sucker growth away from the base of the plant, as this sort of wood will have a tendency to retard development of berry producing branches.

## PITTOSPORUM, SHRUB TYPES
## (tobira, varigated, viridiflorum, etc.)

Although these plants are profuse during the blooming period, with very fragrant flowers, they are grown mainly as foliage shrubs, due to their good compact habit. During recent years the tobira variety has been grown a great deal from seed, and as a result there are a great many off-type plants in the gardens, plants that do not always maintain that compactness for which they are famous. This type of plant will require more attention than the other in the way of thinning, to produce heavier leaf growth. In any stage of this plant's growth, there will be small branches that will shoot out ahead of other growth, beyond the body of the shrub, and these should be cut off to encourage greater solidity. In remov-

77

ing these small branches, cut them well down below the general outline of the foliage. This same thing applies to any of the Pittosporum group of shrub types. This thinning should take place at any time that these offshoots appear, regardless of season.

With the tree forms, such as Crassifolia, undulatum, phillyraeoides or revulutum, train the main stem singly to the height of the desired head of the tree, and from then on the plant will care for itself, with the exception of keeping all suckers pulled off.

The two tall slender growing types, tenuifolia, and eugenoides, will care for themselves without any pruning of any kind.

## PLUMBAGO, white and blue

This is a very hardy, rank growing plant in any location, and will require severe cutting to keep it in good

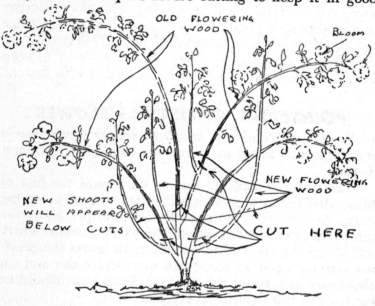

PLUMBAGO — SHOWING METHOD OF
PRUNING OUT OLD WOOD.

bloom. Because of the snarl the branches have a habit of growing into, few people will have the patience to thin out the old wood, that is the best treatment for this plant, but will simply butcher off the entire outside of the plant, all at once. This severe cutting will not do any great harm to the bush, but will leave it rather unsightly for some time.

The right time to do any pruning on the Plumbago is during the winter, while the plant is doing the least growing. Young plants may very easily be gotten into proper shape, but the same system will apply to older specimens. It will be noticed that old branches are very shy of both foliage and bloom clusters, and these should be removed for better results. In taking these old branches out, cut them as far down into the body of the plant as is possible to reach. As much as a third or half of the plant can be removed in this manner without detriment to the appearance, and the results will be striking. The bloom clusters on a well pruned plant of Plumbago will be almost twice the size of those on an untrimmed bush. This cutting out should be done regularly every winter, in order to keep the plant of a constant size, and also loaded with flowers.

## POINSETTIA, CHRISTMAS FLOWER

Pruning of Poinsettias is a very simple process but a very important one if the plants are to produce the finest flowers.

This plant should not be cut back until the first of May, although new growth will be starting all along the stalks. At this time cut the stalks down, to just above the third bud from the bottom of last year's growth. There will always be one bud where the stalk leaves the previous season's wood, so count two buds above this and cut about one inch above the top bud. Each stem should be cut back in this manner, every year.

In the case of very old plants, that have been creeping higher and higher every year, in spite of pruning, cut the entire trunk down to within about one foot of the

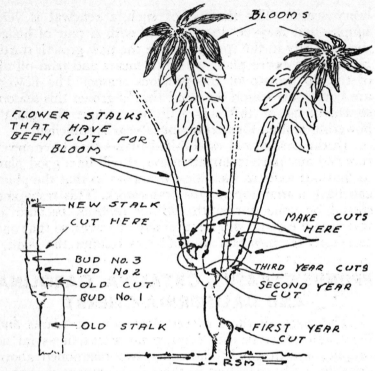

POINSETTIA — SHOWING CUTS TO BE MADE ABOUT MAY FIRST

ground. The Poinsettia is sufficiently hardy that it will overcome even a severe dehorning of this sort.

When the bloom is to be cut for decorative purposes, take whatever of the stem that is required for the purpose and leave the rest to be cut back at the time of pruning. Do not attempt to cut the stem back its full length, when picking the flowers, as this would have a tendency to produce small flowers on these stems instead of perfect specimens.

## POMEGRANATE, DWARF

This little everblooming plant will be short lived unless it is given an opportunity to reproduce new wood every season. The method of such a renewal is very simple, and may be done quickly with a pair of hedge shears. Early in the spring, before the new growth starts, go over the entire plant with the shears and trim off all of the tip growth of the previous season. The flowers are borne this season on wood that is grown this season, so treatment of this sort will not reduce the plant's flowering ability. One trimming a year is sufficient.

In the case of old established plants that have never received any parteicular attention, it will be a good plan to thin out some of the oldest branches so that the plant can have a more open type framework. This reshaping should be done during the winter months, because at this time the shrub will be most shy of leaves, so that one can easily see how best to uniformly reshape the plant.

## PRUNUS CERASUS, CATALINA, CAROLINA AND CALIFORNIA CHERRY

These are all three rather slow growing plants and the California type will require no attention as far as pruning is concerned. The other two mentioned above are sufficiently consistent in their development that they will need little pruning, except to trim off any branch that shows a tendency to pull away from the main form of the top. When this occurs, cut off the branch where it leaves the main body of the plant.

These two latter varieties may be grown into excellent trees when trained to a high head, and allowed to take care of themselves from then on. To give these plants an abundance of water is a mistake that should be avoided. Rapid growth is not desirable for them.

## PYRACANTHA (Cretaegus) FIRETHORN, THORNAPPLE, BURNING BUSH

Within this group of plants are some of our best berry producing plants, as well as being a family that is much abused as to the proper pruning. By caring for your plants according to the system specified below, you will not only prolong the beauty of your bushes, but the plants will produce greater quantities of berries, and keep to a uniform size.

This group, like their sister plants the Cotoneasters, produce their berries on wood that has grown one complete season, and this same wood will not produce another crop. The next season's fruit will keep shoving out further each year unless the plant has the sort of pruning that will make it reproduce in the same area.

All of the Pyracanthas should be pruned as soon as the berries have dropped from the stems, or have become dried. Any plant that is three years old or more should

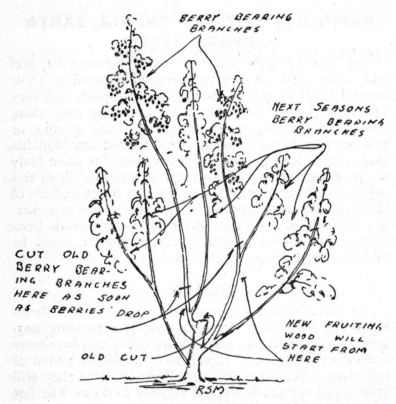

PYRACANTHA — SHOWING RENEWAL METHOD.

have its last year's berry wood cut back every year. Christmas sprays may be cut in plenty, but keep the pruning system in practice when these branches are taken. After a branch has borne one crop of berries, it should be removed and in cutting it out, take it off near the base of the plant, leaving a stub of about six or eight inches in length. From this short stub will spring several shoots, and these will have their crop of berries after one full year's growth. As with many other plants, growth will be decidedly concentrated with the Pyracanthas immediately below any major cut, so if the plant has been "hedged" along the top it will only be a short time before the entire shrub is top-heavy.

## RAPHIOLEPIS, OVATA, INDICA, SANTA BARBARA HYBRID

As a family these are a very well behaved lot, and will require little or no care in regard to pruning. Their natural habit of growth is slow and compact, and very seldom will they need any attention. The only thing which might be suggested to improve their solidity, or to keep them down in height is to thin out any branches that show a tendency to pull away from the main body of the plant with a sudden burst of growth. When this occurs cut the branch off where it leaves the main body of the shrub. These plants are not very susceptible to suckering, so there will be no danger of excess growth from cutting. The flowering ability of the plant can not be improved as a result of pruning.

## ROSES

In this locality, Roses are very apt to wear themselves out with over blooming and by remaining in a growing condition too long a time. They are by nature a deciduous plant, and should have a definite period of rest once a year, but in our milder climates they will grow as an evergreen plant if allowed to do so. The last main crop of bloom will be on the plants about the first of September, and from this time on they should be given no more water until the winter rains soak them and they make their natural start in the spring.

Roses should have a heavy pruning every two winters with a light cutting back every alternate year. This treatment will keep the plants in a good healthy growing condition, which will develop plenty of flower producing wood, providing they receive the proper amount of fertilizer.

By heavy pruning, which should be done every other winter about December first, about two-thirds of the plant's growth is removed, cutting out the oldest wood first, in such a way as to leave the bush evenly balanced with fairly young branches. All new growth should be taken back to within three buds or leaf scars of its base.

When the spring growth starts, there will be danger of suckers springing up from the root stock. This is par-

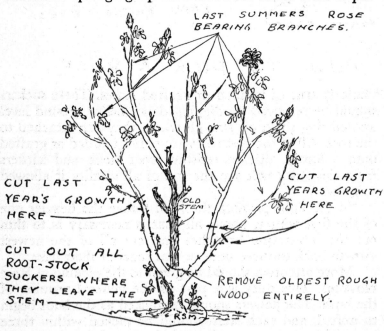

LAST SUMMERS ROSE BEARING BRANCHES.

CUT LAST YEAR'S GROWTH HERE

OLD STEM

CUT LAST YEARS GROWTH HERE

CUT OUT ALL ROOT-STOCK SUCKERS WHERE THEY LEAVE THE STEM

REMOVE OLDEST ROUGH WOOD ENTIRELY.

RSM

BUSH ROSES.

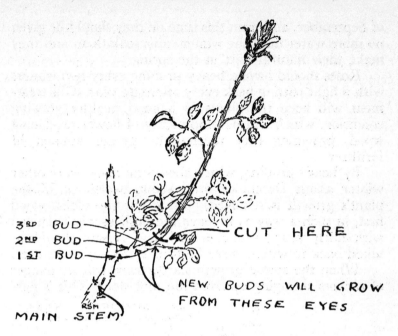

3ᴿᴰ BUD
2ᴺᴰ BUD
1 ST BUD
CUT HERE
NEW BUDS WILL GROW
FROM THESE EYES
MAIN STEM

## HOW TO PICK A ROSE.

ticularly true of budded or grafted Roses. These suckers should be removed by digging down below ground level and cutting them off smooth where they are attached to the root. All of the best roses are either budded or grafted onto a hardy, disease resistant root stock and suckers from this stock will sap the top of all vitality if allowed to grow.

In the light pruning that will follow the heavier one of the first winter, about all that is necessary is to thin out the interfering branches and cut all of the newest growth back to three buds or leaf scars of their base.

More attention should be given to the picking of Rose blossoms. This duty is a part of the general pruning of the bush. The flowers should be picked as the buds begin to unfurl, and each stem should be picked within three buds of its base, regardless of the length of that stem. There will always be one bud at the extreme base of a stem, so count two buds or leaf scars above this one and cut the flower stem just above this last bud.

Roses should never be allowed to produce seed as this production reduces the flowering ability of the plant. In removing them, follow the same system as one would in picking a flower, in order to make way for additional flower wood. Good quality roses will not be borne from the buds farther out on the stems, so do not think that you can get more and better flowers by leaving more than the above mentioned three buds.

Fertilize your Roses according to the soil in your own yard, and the locality in which you live, and follow the directions above for their pruning, and the results will be worth while.

## SALVIA, SAGE

The Salvia leucantha, or Purple Sage, being a deciduous variety, or one that sheds its leaves, requires very simple treatment. The flowers are borne on current season stems, or that is, stems that grow this season will produce flowers this season, and when these stems have flowered once, they are through as far as flowering is concerned. During the winter these old stems should be cut off down to the ground, which will allow the root to send up an entirely new crop of flower stems.

The other more common varieties that are found among gardens are of the herbaceous or shrubby type, and inclined to grow very open and unsightly in a few seasons. When they reach this stage, they should be cut back heavily all over the entire plant, removing all branches down to about eight or ten inches from the ground. They will quickly recover.

Other types of this plant that have a perennial root and annual top, will take care of themselves. The tops will die off every winter, and new shoots come up in the spring to replace them.

*Have Your Nurseryman*
*Identify Your Plants*

## SHADE TREES

The primary training of a srade tree is of the greatest importance, and should be given particular attention during the first three or four years of their growth. A tree incorrectly started will never get over the bad effects of its early training.

The first thing to consider in the training of a shade tree, is a good straight trunk. This has to be done, in the

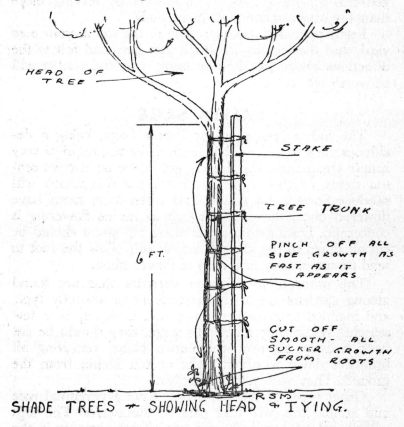

HEAD OF TREE

STAKE

TREE TRUNK

PINCH OFF ALL SIDE GROWTH AS FAST AS IT APPEARS

6 FT.

CUT OFF SMOOTH - ALL SUCKER GROWTH FROM ROOTS

-RSM-

SHADE TREES → SHOWING HEAD & TYING.

great majority of cases, by tying the main stem to a stake or iron pipe. Two inch square material should be used as a stake. In tying the stem to the stake, always remember the tying is a guide, not a support. Tie the string or tape tight around the *stake,* then loosely around the stem of the plant. This type of tying will prevent binding of the growth as it expands, and also encourage the plant to develop some strength of its own. A branch will develop strength as that quality is required of the wood, and if the need for strength is done away with, by tying too tight or putting a prop under a limb, sufficient strength will never be developed. All that tying should do for the tree is to keep it growing in a generally straight direction. Slight variations, or waviness in the stem will be outgrown as the trunk develops. Place the tying guides about one foot apart, and have them sufficiently loose to allow a movement of at least three inches either way.

The second important item in the training of a shade tree is to establish the height of head, or the distance that lower limbs are to be from the ground. For all practical purposes no limbs should be allowed below a height of six feet. When a small tree is planted out, allow nothing but the tip or terminal bud to develop. Any side or lateral branches should be pinched off as soon as they are formed. These lateral branches will usually come out at the axil or base of a leaf, and when the tender shoot is pinched off, do not remove the leaf with it. Leaves are very essential to the rapid growth of any plant. Keep up this pinching off of lateral growth until the top has reached a height of six feet, and from then on the tree will shape itself.

Some varieties are easily blown one sided by a prevailing wind, and where this is known before planting, the trunk should be trained into the wind at a considerable angle. Where a growing tree is becoming one-sided from wind, do not try to tie back or to straighten it artificially, because in event that the support breaks at some later date, the whole tree will usually go down as a result of being weakened from outside support. Trees that are wind blown in this manner should be trimmed out on the lower part of the heavy side, which will force new growth on the light side, and in this way the tree may be straightened up without weakening the general structure of the plant.

As shade trees become older, the lower branches will gradually come down, until they interfere in some way. This is only a natural thing, and is caused by the weight of leaves and wood year after year. Do not prop these branches up and try to save them. By sawing them off wherever they become an interference, new growth will be formed higher up in the tree. With some trees, it is very noticeable, this constant lowering of the under limbs, and the constant renewal of limbs higher in the tree which in turn gradually come down. By the time these lower branches have lowered sufficiently to necessitate removal they have passed their days of usefulness to the

SHADE TREES — SHOWING REMOVAL OF LOWERING BRANCHES — DO NOT USE PROPS

tree, so their being cut away will not harm the physical structure of the plant.

There are some trees that are planted mainly because of their rapid growth, and this one fact makes them very unsatisfactory as a shade tree of long life. Typical of this group are the Acacias. They are very fast growers and have a reputation for short life, and a weak anchorage from their roots. These bad points may be overcome to some extent by proper training while they are young. When the Acacia reaches a height of ten feet or more, the growth is liable to be so fast that they will send out long ungainly shoots of weak structure. These should be cut back about three-fourths their length, and should be done at the end of each summer, until the tree develops a good massive head, and stops sending out these long awkward growths. Treatment of this sort will also give the tree an opportunity to grow a sturdier root system, and one that is not so liable to give way the first time a heavy wind follows a good rain.

## SPIREA, BRIDAL WREATH

The deciduous varieties of Spirea may all be treated alike, as far as pruning is concerned. They all have the same habits of growth. The evergreen variety will be taken up in the last part of these directions.

Depending on the location and care under which the Bridal Wreath is grown, there is no set age at which this plant should be pruned for the first time. It all depends upon the size of the plant, and pruning may begin, depending on the shrub, any time after it is three years old. Pruning should take place as soon as the flowers have dropped in the spring.

The best flowers are produced on young wood, and care should be exercised to keep the older wood cut out and new flowering branches coming on. While the shrub is in full bloom, it can be noticed that the oldest stems, the ones having the greatest diameter, are the ones bearing the least flowers. These branches should be cut out as soon as the petals have dropped. Cut them well down to their base, leaving a short stub of about six inches. New shoots will form on these stubs, and will be flowering themselves in the following spring. Some of the Spireas become very spreading, and in such cases the most extreme spreading branches should be trimmed close to the ground to encourage as much center growth as possible.

The Evergreen Spirea, or Spirea anthony waterer, requires an entirely different type of pruning, and is

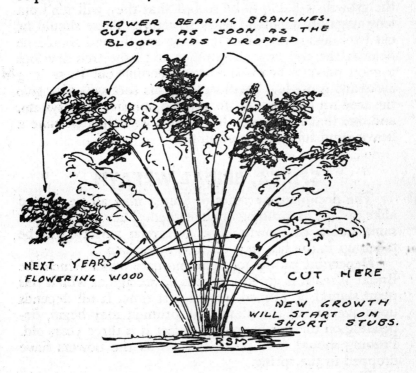

SPIREA (DECIDUOUS) — SHOWING METHOD OF REMOVING OLD FLOWERING WOOD.

carried on through the summer months, while the plant is in bloom. The best flower clusters are borne at the ends of the branches. The secondary bloom, or that which grows out from the side buds after the main flower has been fully developed, will not be as large a cluster, nor will it show up much on the plant due to the fact that it is down in the body of the shrub. This secondary bloom should not be considered. As soon as the main flower has dried, cut the entire stem upon which this was borne down towards its base, leaving a short stub of about three inches. New shoots will appear upon these stubs, and in time will make flowering stems.

The cream and pink varigations that cause the leaves to turn such peculiar colors, are natural, and will come and go throughout the life of the plant.

## STREPTOSOLEN JAMESONI

Due to the fact that this plant is quite tender to frost, it is not found generally throughout this locality. But where it may be grown it can be kept a riot of color all through its blooming period, if the right sort of flowering wood is developed.

It is natural for this plant to throw sucker growth readily, and this wood will produce the largest and most beautiful clusters of bloom. To get the best results, one should encourage this sucker wood as much as possible by trimming out the oldest branches after they have been on the plant three full years. Branches that remain on the shrub too long a time will not put out the best flowers that can be grown. In cutting out these branches, follow down the stem and cut them out about eight inches from the ground. New growth will appear on the stub that has been left. This treatment will also keep the plant in better foliage.

This shrub is by nature very drooping, and because of this, it should not be tied up unless absolutely necessary. By pruning out the lowest hanging branches which will encourage new inside shoots, one can remedy the too pendulous habit more permanently.

Lack of pruning on this variety will often result in a short lived plant. The life of this shrub may be increased several years by making it possible for new wood to be forced out every year.

## TETRAPANAX PAPYRIFERUM (Aralia Papyriferum), RICEPAPER PLANT

Wherever this plant will thrive at all one will find that the growth is very rank, requiring some sort of control measure very often.

If when the plant is young the main stem is cut off about three feet from the ground, new shoots will be forced out all along the stem, which will make for a larger top and a much more beautiful plant. Let as many of these new shoots develop as the plant will throw out.

Old plants of this variety are very apt to become top-heavy, due to the weak character of the trunk. When they begin to show signs of doing this, the main stem should be cut back heavily, or if there should happen to be shoots, lower down on the stem, the main stem can be cut off just above one of these shoots. Even though the trunk is cut down to nothing but a stub, there will be no danger of the plant dying, as it is exceptionally hardy.

Late spring or early summer will be the best time of year to do any heavy cutting.

## TIBOUCHINA SEMIDECANDRA, PLEROMA, PRINCESS FLOWER

This shrub presents rather a problem regarding its pruning, because cutting back is very necessary to its well-being, and this same cutting back usually disfigures the plant for quite awhile.

The best bloom will always appear on the fast growing tips of branches, and in order to get the largest possible flowers, these branches must be growing rapidly, and this condition can be best brought about by not allowing the plant to grow to more than a four foot height. In order to keep this growing habit at its best, it is advisable to cut back a branch that has reached this

93

height, well down into the body of the shrub. Make the cut about one-halfinch above a bud or joint in the stem. This pruning may be done at any time of the year.

Pruning the plant in this manner will leave quite a

THIN OUT
TALLEST
GROWTH HERE
TO FORCE
NEW GROWTH
HERE.

CUT OUT
LOWERING
BRANCHES
HERE

## TIBOUCHINA.
### PRINCESS FLOWER.          PLEROMA.

hole, but it will soon be filled in with other growth. The lowering, outer branches may be pruned off from time to time as needed, when they are dragging on the ground.

Keeping this plant to a four-foot height is recommended because its branches do not have sufficient strength to support taller growth without the necessity of being tied up during winds and rain.

## VERONICA

The only varieties of this plant that will require any

attention in the way of pruning are the ones used as flowering plants, such as andersoni, imperialis, eliptica, or deccussata, rosea or carnea, and others. The herbaceous types will not need any definite system of cutting back.

With the above mentioned types, the pruning should be carried on all through the flowering season for the best results. The best flowers will appear at the tip of vigorous branches, and although there would be other flower spikes later on, the best quality of bloom will be produced if one will clip off these flower producing stems as soon as the flower has dried. In removing these stems, they should be cut out well down in the body of the plants, leaving about three joints or old leaf scars between the cut and the base of the stem.

With this sort of care the plant may be kept at about the same size all the time, and there will be much more first class flowers on the plant than if it is allowed to go uncared for. About once every two years it will be necessary, with some of the dense, low growing types, to cut away some of the branches that are down on the ground. These branches rarely set flowers, and they will often take root, causing the parent plant to spread all out of bounds.

## VIBURNUM, EVERGREEN TYPES

In this group are included several plants that are used primarily as foliage plants, and as such will require little in the way of pruning, except to thin them out as they become too large for the location in which they have been planted.

This reshaping of the plant should be done during the winter months, and is accomplished by selecting several of the longer branches, spaced evenly throughout. Cut them off well down into the body of the plant, which will cause new growth to be forced lower down on the branches.

In some cases, these plants will become rather open in growth, due possibly to one of several circumstances, and in such cases the shrub may be thickened up, by clipping off some of the more prominent tips of branches all over the outside of the shrub. This will result in new shoots starting throughout the entire plant and in a short time the foliage will be greatly increased.

## WEIGELIA, ALL VARIETIES

After this plant has reached an age of three years it will require pruning every season for the best results. The finest flowers will be borne on branches that have had at least one full summer's growth. Pruning should be done as soon as the plant has stopped flowering, which is in most cases early summer. Due to the fact that some varieties continue to bloom quite late in the spring and early summer, it is impossible to do necessary pruning of the old flowering shoots by next spring. However, when a branch is old enough to produce the best flowers it will do so, and when this crop of bloom has been produced, that branch should be cut out. Cut these branches well down to their base, leaving a stub of about six or eight inches. New growth will form on these stubs.

## WILLOWS

All of the Willow family that are grown as ornamental trees will require very heavy cutting in order to keep them within bounds, and particularly the Pussy Willow.

The best Catkins of the Pussy Willow will be borne on new wood, and this type of growth should be renewed every year for the best results. Pruning should be done every spring as soon as the branchlets have put out their crop of flower buds, or Catkins. All of the past season's growth should be cut back to its base, leaving a short stub of two or three inches in length. The next season's Catkins will be borne upon the growth that will appear on these short stubs.

Pruning of this nature will cause the plant to become more and more bushy every year, and will greatly prolong the natural life of your Pussy Willow.